Building My Zen Garden

Building My Zen Garden

❧

Kieran Egan

A Frances Tenenbaum Book

Houghton Mifflin Company

Boston New York 2000

For information about permission to reproduce selections from this book,
write to Permissions, Houghton Mifflin Company, 215 Park Avenue South,
New York, New York 10003.

Visit our Web site: www.houghtonmifflinbooks.com.

Library of Congress Cataloging-in-Publication Data
Egan, Kieran.
  Building my Zen garden / Kieran Egan.
    p. cm.
  "A Frances Tenenbaum book."
  ISBN 0-618-06378-1
  1. Gardens, Japanese—Zen influences—Design and construction. I. Title.
SB458.E36 2000
712'.6'0952—dc21   00-056710

Printed in the United States of America

Book design by Lisa Diercks
The text of this book is typeset in Columbus (Monotype).

QUM 10 9 8 7 6 5 4 3 2 1

The author is grateful for permission to reprint lines from *The Jade Mountain,* by
Witter Bynner, trans. Copyright 1929 and renewed 1957 by Alfred A. Knopf Inc.
Reprinted by permission of Alfred A. Knopf, a Division of Random House Inc.

To Joshua Ciarán Egan and Jordan Kató Egan

Contents

Building My Zen Garden

Introduction

I VISITED JAPAN FOR THE first time last summer, and stayed with a friend whose partner had converted the small balcony of their apartment into a miniature Japanese garden. It was a miracle of design and made what might otherwise have been a dull few square meters into a treat for the eye and spirit. The small garden was augmented gradually by stones "liberated" from sites around Nagoya or farther afield. This meant that a drive might at any moment be interrupted as Tanya's eagle eye spotted an appropriately shaped stone by the side of a field or in a back alley or in some more precarious spot. The car would lurch to a halt, and Mike and Tanya would look around with that exaggerated casualness I last saw in 1950s British movies as the only-too-obvious villain prepared to grab the unsuspecting dowager's diamonds. Mike would climb out, examine the sky for a few moments while edging closer to the stone, and then with a swift lunge and grunt would heave it into the back of the car. Later, in the apartment, the stones would be cleaned and carefully set to enhance the accumulating beauty of the balcony garden. They were also coated with yogurt, which encourages bacterial growth and so the illusion of immemorial years of serene repose on the seventh-floor balcony of the modern high-rise.

When I returned home to Vancouver in Canada, I considered

trying to emulate Tanya's transformation on our back deck. But our wide North American decks don't seem well suited to that particular form of beautification. Looking at the wreck of the rear of our garden a while later, I thought I could try to create a Japanese garden there. It was a wreck because the fence at the back was one of those old green plastic mesh affairs and it backed onto the one neglected corner of our adjoining neighbor's otherwise well-tended garden. Their shrubs had spotted my reluctance for confrontation and invaded with manic enthusiasm, carrying the mesh fence with them as a cunning disguise of just how much ground they were expanding into. The area is also surrounded by trees, with too little sunlight for a successful lawn. It had become, over the years, a neglected strip behind one of those lumberyard playhouses I had bought and constructed by numbers when our three children were little.

So I had my spot. I would make a Japanese garden along the back strip between the fence of our neighbors to the north, the compost containers I had built a few years ago to the south, the playhouse to the west, and the green mesh fence to the east. This gave me a space of about 40 feet along the back of the garden, by about 15 feet. I suspected my wife would be reluctant to authorize further encroachment into the "real" garden. Ours is a typical suburban lot of 45 feet by 170 feet, with the traditional English-style lawn surrounded by a border of flowers and shrubs.

The trouble with taking on any large task is that there seem to be so many things one has to do before one can do what one wants, and then things to do before one can do the things before the things one wants. The other trouble with this project was that what I had initially imagined as a small strip with some stones, perhaps a raised area with plants and a decorative Japanese lantern, gradually grew in my imagination. The plan soon included a pond with a small stream and waterfall, and a teahouse/scholar's study with a veranda over the pond.

When I say the plan, I don't mean that I first sat down and carefully drew up a plan. I know that is what one is supposed to do. After the project was under way, guests might ask (politely, indulgently, resignedly, even one or two, I think, interestedly) to see the work-in-progress, and many, unenchanted by the mounds of earth and gravel and the untidy hole that was to be the pond, asked if they might see the plan. At first I was discomfited by such requests. I felt guilty that I couldn't unroll sharp lined blueprints, showing elevations and the "artist's impressions" of the completed landscape. My plan was just that I imagined the raised garden at one end—raised to create a run for a pump-driven stream—and the pond in the middle, where the stream might fall, and the teahouse at the other side. That was the plan, and I basically made each element up as I went along. That makes it seem very casual, but I didn't know enough about what might be involved in the construction of each part to make a more elaborate plan. If I had, of course, I would never have begun. I just wanted to make a beautiful place, such as Tanya had, with the added attraction that I would be able to sit peacefully in it.

That is, I set out in a rather indirect and rambling way to make a paradise. It seems the ancient Persian rulers built, as an essential part of their palaces, a walled garden. The *pairidaeza* was a protected area within which one might create something, and *pairi* is also the source of our word "dairy." The Greek version of the word was used in the Bible for the Garden of Eden. The connection between gardens and paradise, then, is of long standing in human languages and imaginations. It is our ideal cooperation with nature. We create forms within which nature does its thing to our mutual satisfaction. In my own haphazard way I wanted to create what it would be tacky to call the garden of Egan.

That notion of our ideal cooperation with nature was an assumption I began with but found myself increasingly wondering about. A theme of much Zen writing, as of the Bible, is that human beings are aware something is not quite right in our relations with the natural world. The garden is an ambivalent arena in which we try somehow to cure or disguise the problem. I found myself constantly caught up in that ambivalence as I worked, nature seeming an implacable foe as much as a cooperator in creating harmony.

The first task—instead of beginning on the garden, or building the fence I decided to put up to protect the garden from invading shrubs—was to take down the old playhouse. It was beginning to show its age—about twenty years or so —and likely wouldn't be altogether safe by the time our grandchildren would be ready to use it. After beginning the clearing and taking down the swing and part of the playhouse, I thought I should try to record the process in pictures, as no doubt your average Persian emperor would have done had he had a Minolta.

In the first picture, the wild shrubs pushing the mesh fence are to the left; directly ahead, shaded, is the compost heap that supports my wife's flowers and my vegetable garden, and the shed that I also built by numbers some years ago. I took the photo from where I imagine the teahouse will stand; the near ends of the lumber on the lawn are where the pond is to go; and the playhouse itself is where the raised garden is supposed to rise. To the east there is the riotous shrubbery that ceases across from the distant end of the playhouse. At that point, the neighbors' garden ends and that of a condominium begins. What you can't see in the picture is a large birch tree that grows in the rear corner of the condominium lot and hangs over the site where I want to build my Zen garden. Negotiations with the management committee feature in my struggle to make a pond where fish might be happy.

My aim is to describe the process I followed in building, from a weedy and more or less waste 40' × 15' chunk of

The original site, looking south, with the old playhouse coming down.

garden, an attractive place with the qualities traditionally sought by Japanese gardeners — beauty, tranquillity, and harmony. While I focus on this single construction in a particular place, I have tried to include the principles I learned and have also discussed the choices I did not make. Thus the book is a useful general guide to constructing a small garden using more or less Japanese principles (which I present as the building goes forward). There are compromises with Western notions here and there, in part as matters of choice, in part due to the materials or plants that were available or that I could afford.

But the Japanese garden itself seems to have been a kind of compromise. During the T'ang dynasty (c. A.D. 600–900) a fashion developed among some Chinese poets and painters to withdraw from the city to a rural retreat. There they would

The original site, looking north. To the right is the chaos that my fence needs to inhibit from further encroachment; ahead is the area where the the teahouse will stand. I imagine it on stilts, raised up a few feet. I'm not sure why—perhaps I always wanted a tree house or saw the film version of *The Swiss Family Robinson* at a too impressionable age.

live in isolation, preferably in the mountains, near running water, working on their art. "Isolation" for these wealthy men might include a retinue of twenty servants and an adequate number of concubines. One may see paintings of their "huts" in the mountains in which they sit contemplating nature while servants bustle around taking care of everything that might prove to be a distraction. The rural concealment, ironically, often stimulated interest in the artist's work and brought fame and exposure to large audiences.

In the later T'ang period and into the Sung dynasty (c. 900–1300) the first compromise involved those who wanted the sublime environment as an aid to contemplation and a stimulant to painting or poetry, but who did not fancy the idea of heading for a hut in the hills. They began to replicate the wild environments of stones and water, of evergreen trees and grasses, within their walled city estates. This construction of stylized wilderness gardens in town became a fashion among wealthy civil servants.

The further compromise involved the Japanese importing this fashion in artificial wilderness gardening, to which they added the element of the tea ceremony and the teahouse. The teahouse is a replication of the Chinese artists' huts of centuries before, and the tea ceremony is a ritualized recreation of the contemplative condition the mountain fastness was supposed to induce. So my desire to build something closer to a study than a traditional teahouse simply hearkens back to an older tradition.

Spiritual ideals inspire the design and building of Japanese gardens. Along with the style of garden and the semi-religious purpose of creating a sense of harmony, respect, purity, and tranquillity (*wa, kei, sei,* and *jaku*), the Japanese also inherited from the Chinese a penumbra of Zen and Taoist ideas and stories related to the elements of the garden. I draw on these where appropriate, inserting them among the details of hacking roots, mixing concrete, heaving stones around, and bolting 2" × 8"s to 4" × 4"s. Perhaps I can begin here with Chuang Tzu, who was walking by a pond with a friend one day:

> "How delightfully the fish are enjoying themselves in the water," exclaimed Chuang Tzu.
> "You are not a fish," said his friend. "How can you know they are enjoying themselves!"
> "You are not me," replied Chuang Tzu. "How can you know that I do not know that the fish are enjoying themselves?"

My planning has been largely a matter of looking through books; mostly from the library, a few bought, one splendidly illustrated Japanese book (in English), a present from the friend whose partner began all this. The books are invaluable for getting ideas and seeing possibilities, but can be intimidating. The American books typically illustrate how "workers" dressed in flawless white trousers and unscuffed tan shoes dig out a pond or build a retaining wall using manicured soil off which you would willingly eat breakfast. The first Japanese book I read (in translation) began with the master gardener discussing clothing. His first advice was not to work in old clothes. Rather, one should have a special gardening outfit, or, I suppose, two for when the first is in the wash. I began to feel I was already involved in uncivilized Western compromises. The old jeans and shirts it was going to be.

What stimulated this megaproject—apart from the aesthetic pleasure created by Tanya's example and looking for an activity that would give me physical exercise, keep me off the streets, and provide a break from a job that requires sitting at a desk for much of each day—is the image of being in the tea-house/study looking across at the tranquil garden and down at the pond, with the silky sound of black bamboo moving in the breeze. And the slightly mad dream that in this environment of water, stones, and green plants I will be able to capture the winged words that elude me in the more utilitarian environments in which I currently write. An ironic conclusion will no doubt see me sitting in this manufactured paradise, unable to write another lousy word—as Dylan Thomas feelingly put it— either bemused by the sensuous beauty and calm of the place, or too exhausted and broken-bodied by the building process itself. But if I can't write my own winged words, I will have created a pleasant place in which to read other people's.

And what will I write in this perfected repose? If I knew that, I wouldn't be out there digging and nailing and fiddling with pumps and heaving stones around. I have been writing academic books for years and would like a change, writing something in which the imagination can have freer play. But I can think about it as I heave the stones. Perhaps some lapidary poems.

It would, of course, have made the ideal place in which to write this book. I began by simply writing a bit of text to accompany the pictures I was putting on my World Wide Web home page. Then I found some of the incidents either odd or funny and the text became more elaborate. Some kind people said they were enjoying the story, and so I extended it further and then took the plunge of packaging the bits I had then written and sending them off to a literary agent. She was, to my surprise, enthusiastic about it and sent it to a publisher, who accepted it. So I found myself in the odd situation of having two projects instead of one. They haven't always happily co-existed, even though the struggles and rewards of garden building and book building have some features in common.

But in the teahouse/study I can sit at the end of it all and read Zen sages, and no doubt slowly learn from them how I would better have embodied their wisdom by not beginning this frantic Western plan to shape the world to some seductive image taken from books. Instead I should have cultivated *wan wei*—the acceptance of the world as it is. The message of the sages is that I should not have done all this in the first place. But I will have to manage the irony that if I had not done it, I would never have learned that I should not have done it.

And what am I doing building a Zen garden on the west coast of Canada anyway? It began, as I said, as a simple aesthetic response to my friend's partner's balcony garden. I set about it somewhat whimsically, edging half unconsciously into the practical work. And it became, in a peculiar journey of discovery on which I hope you will join me, a slow gathering of understanding about the principles that give form and meaning to distinctively Japanese gardens and to a Zen stance in the world. Why a Zen garden, rather than, say, an extension of our English garden? I have no idea, though an uninformed, romantic image of black bamboo gracefully bowing in the rain played a part.

Another impulse leading into this unexpected enterprise was perhaps the distant memory of my grandfather gardening when I was a small boy in Ireland. Later, as a student, I lived in upstate New York for a few years, renting a house with a derelict vegetable garden attached. I remember going out in the spring with a spade, thinking that I would prepare the ground for seeds. I stood with my foot on the spade, and realized I didn't even know how to dig. Did I put the soil I pulled up on top of the earth ahead, or turn it over into the hole? Slowly I worked it out, and after an hour or so found that I had precisely replicated the raised vegetable beds my grandfather used to build. They were ideal for the wet Irish climate, but perhaps not so well suited to upstate New York. I have continued putting in a simple vegetable garden each year and have since realized that what I most enjoy is making beautifully raked and symmetrical raised beds. In fact, I get rather bored thereafter with the business of putting seeds in and weeding, though I do enjoy eating the product, if it is not taken over by weeds by the time it's ready for harvesting. So, I don't bring a history of dedicated gardening to this task of building my Zen garden, but do seem to bring an old impulse to move earth around.

The stereotype of Irishness may not seem ideally suited to the pacific harmony characteristic of the Japanese garden. And as the project goes forward, conflicts between my Irish impulsiveness and unplanned casualness and Japanese meticulousness, precision, and care erupt in occasional mayhem, psychological chaos, and interesting compromises.

Bear in mind, though, that the patron saint of gardening, St. Fiacre, is Irish. St. Fiacre, fourteenth in descent (one needs to know!) from Conn of the Hundred Battles, king of Ireland from 523 to 577, died in France in 670. He grew herbs, and believed water and stone were essential to a good garden. He encouraged his disciples to garden in order to produce food for the poor, and to nourish their souls in contemplation as they dealt with the ultimate realities so apparent when one turns over a spadeful of earth.

The fence, the quince, and the black bamboo

MY FIRST CLOSE LOOK AT
the shrubbery aggressing into the area where I was to build
the Zen garden was not encouraging. The major bulk of the
invasion was fronted by the exuberantly expanding forsythia,
sending a multitude of new shoots in spreading clumps that
clearly found my side of the fence infinitely more hospitable
than their own. Adding density to the advancing front were
twisting strands of the dreaded wild bindweed (*Convolvulus
sepium,* apparently), well characterized by its common name.
It had run amuck, huge white flowers defying one to dislike
it or, at least, making one feel guilty for wanting to destroy it.
As I poked around, I found a mass of its writhing roots—one
of its English names is, appropriately, "devil's guts"—in a deep
mound of ash where our neighbors had dumped their barbe-
cue leavings for the past two hundred years. An attractive but
ubiquitous dark green ivy contributed to the appearance of
daunting impenetrability. And adding a prickly and aggressive
edge to this nasty brigade were sturdy thumb-thick stalks of
a wild blackberry. One stalk had somehow managed to take
off from the top of the forsythia and get a tendril attached to

our distant pear tree. It was dropping a searching tip that was beginning to root itself into our lawn. Perhaps, I reflected with uneasy premonitions, it would be easier to take up some other project — growing bonsai or bird watching.

I had to shift from planning the garden itself to thinking what kind of fence might be able to hold back these determined floral desperadoes. They were supported by battalions of the sneakier weeds that propagate prodigiously by sending out underground rhizomes of supernatural and malevolent cunning, along with a paler ivy of Amazonian fertility and metallic toughness, all thickened and interwoven with a riot of anonymous but determined rainforest bioforms.

One stimulus to gardening, which maybe one wants not to acknowledge, is that it is as close as humans get to creation, to making a world of stone, water, plants, and so on — a smaller-scale Earth. The gardener presumes to become God-like. And like the God of the Creation, we want to make a paradise. Our paradises need boundaries, fences, to separate that wilderness beyond our control from the area where we can attempt to work a compromise with nature. Even the Garden of Eden had a fence, through whose gates Adam and Eve were expelled by the angel with the flaming sword. But yet, paradoxically, in the Zen tradition the whole universe is contained in each of its parts, and the garden is a part of the whole that is the world, wilderness and all.

The fence marks a barrier, but we must recognize that it is artificial. We are intruding on nature, making a crass human mark across nature's continuities. One principle of Japanese gardening requires us respectfully to disguise our intrusions, harmonizing what is on our side of the fence with what is beyond. The ideal garden will succeed in two diametrically opposed objectives: to cut off one's created paradise from the rest of the regrettably imperfect world, and yet to suggestively include within one's creation whatever is outside its boundaries.

The Japanese call it "borrowing scenery," suggesting that one's garden continues into what is beyond it. What is beyond, in this case, is the overgrown riot, but also trees and some tall shrubs, and I must think what I can put in place to soften the intrusion of my fence into this surrounding flora. Bamboo will help to reflect the greenery beyond and also soften the sharp lines of the fence. And the neighbor's japonica quince, delicate red flowers showing despite clinging ivy and branch-high weeds, will need protection during my affront on the matted overgrowth, and will, later on but happily, become duplicated on my side of the fence.

Good fences make good neighbors. Love your neighbor, but don't take down your fence (although Robert Frost had his doubts). Well, there's that too, but the Japanese concern is not just with property limits and getting along with others, but reminds us always to be attentive to the rhythms and slow dark music of that most significant other, nature. The spirit of gardening is a cooperation with nature. But we need to recognize, even while we attempt to cooperate, that nature has made no promises to cooperate in return, and will resist us with slow, remorseless energy.

Clearing some space

My fence, my gross intrusion, was to serve as a barrier against the invasion of the neighboring wilderness and be the necessary limit that any paradise requires. And so I had to amass the resources of human ingenuity to clear the ground. The most gratifyingly effective tools were a simple pair of pruning shears and the wonderfully destructive mattock. I thought I had bought a pickax, till a friend with a farming background referred to it as a mattock. It has a sharp pick at one side of the head, and an adzlike flat blade at the other.

How to begin? As soon as I approached any part of the thicket, something tried to poke me in the eye or grab my sweater or trouser legs with its thorns. I started with the pruning shears where the condominium fence ended and the thicket began, just snipping the reachable ends of everything that jutted over my side of the line. This was no doubt enormously wasteful of time, but I wasn't in a hurry. I was more interested, for this first foray, to get some sense of what I was up against. It was slow and pleasant work; and what I was up against was an enemy that knew time was on its side and seemed to sneer at these early attempts to throw back its front-rank troops.

I snipped and cut, and occasionally struggled to sever bits of thick forsythia, pulled out chunks of bindweed, and particularly tried to free the green plastic mesh fence from the vines and branches that entangled it. After a few sweaty hours, I had covered maybe as much as four feet, and had an accumulating mound of fronds and stems and branches in a pile on the lawn. I was making progress, if only in discovering how matted and tenacious were some of the deeply clotted forts of the enemy. Ah, but my slow and cautious maneuvering was really part of a larger strategy to lull the more resilient of my foes into a false sense of security. They could confuse this tidy snipping with an invigorating pruning, not realizing that I was just clearing space to wield the mattock like an Irish berserker.

After a few hours the next day, I had released about six feet of the old green mesh fence, and pulled it out and down onto the lawn. The four-foot-tall posts to which it was attached came down with it, rotted through at the base, and carried forward by the invading horde. A couple more sessions and the mesh was completely released, rolled up, and ready for the dump.

I nailed U-shaped fasteners to the fence posts at either end of the stretch where I was going to build, and tied a bright yellow string between them, using a carpenter's level to make it . . . well, level. Being a bookish person, I have tended most to admire cleverness in words and ideas. But working on this project has made me again and again want to shout with admiration at the practical ingenuity of tool inventors. In their wonder, beauty, and brilliant simplicity, so many tools are surely as close to perfection as humans have managed. The carpenter's level exploits water's convenient inclination to lie flat against the surface of the earth. Chuang Tzu notes that "among level things, water at rest is the most perfect." How more perfectly for our practical building purposes could that perfection be used than in the carpenter's level?

The level yellow string marked a clear line against which I could site the new posts for my fence. It also showed how much more of the thicket I had to cut back. The depressing part was looking down at the ground and seeing what a mass of coagulated stems and roots remained on my side of the line.

This was the point when I realized that all those millennia of experiments with metals and alloys, from ancient Sumeria to the Industrial Revolution, hadn't been a waste of time. Wielding the mattock, I cleared in an afternoon what would have taken a prehistoric village a month. The dense stems of the forsythia crumbled, and the adz blade ripped out the roots with ease. Occasionally a twig lashed at me as it fell, and things with thorns snatched at whatever they could reach.

But the power of the mattock was intoxicating. It struck with satisfying carnage. Sweating and sticky, I lifted the heavy tool over my head and swung again and again. It sheared through everything in sight. Knotted clumps of roots, which I had poked at ineffectually with a spade, exploded under the mighty mattock. Luckily I started midafternoon in the early spring. Had darkness not called me to my senses, I might have hacked my way across town. Alas, destruction is deliriously more dramatic, with its seductive satisfactions, than construction.

I realize that this destructive zeal isn't quite in keeping with the ideals of pacific harmony the Japanese garden is designed to produce in my soul. No doubt one of the Zen masters has a paradoxical observation about violence leading to calm, like Samson's riddle about strength producing sweetness, or the repose that follows storms, but requires the storms for the repose to follow.

What leaves one guilty in such destructive triumphs is that the plants seem so unrecriminating. They are just biding their time. Already I was beginning to sense that the romantic partnership between the gardener and nature was really no such thing. It may seem a partnership only because the weaker and more temporary partner claims it is; but the other partner is utterly committed to anarchy and wildness and the long, long view, arching beyond our temporary intrusions.

You might be wondering what the neighbors with whom we shared that boundary thought of my heroic slashing and ripping of their forsythia and other flora. Fortunately for me, they had moved out, razed the house, and were selling their lot. Unfortunately for them, they set about this at the point when an economic downturn led to a dive in the local real estate market, and no one was showing much interest in buying. On the "It's an ill wind . . ." principle, this meant I could hack away with some impunity at the overgrown shrubs, and helps explains why they were overgrown. The neighbors occasionally came back to prevent their lot from growing too wild, too "natural"; and Shirley, who had built the garden over a quarter of a century, assured me it would be fine to slash away, as new owners would likely level the whole site anyway.

Beginning the fence

While engaged in this assault on the thicket, I was also having to decide what kind of fence I would put up along the line of cleared ground to hold off further encroachments—under way, I realized, millimeter by millimeter from the moment I stopped for the day. I wouldn't like you to think I took this battle personally, but as I lay down to sleep or sat reading with a cup of coffee after work, I would be conscious that the wilderness was out there with nothing else to do but grow. And do it most energetically in the direction of my garden. At night I imagined listening to the ground with a supersensitive ear. Roots would be squeezing through soil, scraping past stones, sucking nutrients. If one could hear these faintest noises, one would know the tumultuous, ceaseless energy of these aggressors. The peace we have sitting in our gardens comes only because our hearing is so dull. We think of plants as silent, but they make a riot of the first foot or so of soil.

And they would be noisiest of all in spring. Spring is usually associated with hope, with light and color, with a general picking up of the spirit after the pretend death of winter. But when building a garden, one cannot escape the unstoppable inexorability of spring. Regardless of one's schedules, it won't wait. T. S. Eliot noted that April is the cruelest month. One needs to bear in mind, among the romantic lushness, the appealing astringency of Dorothy Parker's "Every year, back comes Spring, with nasty little birds yapping their fool heads off and the ground all mucked up with plants."

On days when it rained, I would search for pictures of fences that looked distinctively Japanese. Most of the fences pictured in the books were made of bamboo, usually tied together with knots of supernatural complexity. I think I had measles when they did knots at the Boy Scouts, and I never really caught up. Also, I didn't know where I would be able to buy those sturdy bamboo canes locally. Another problem with many of the books about Japanese gardens, from my perspective, is that the authors assume you are landscaping the back fifty—acres, rather than square yards—and have a squad of skilled workers to call on. A half-dozen clever-fingered experts in bamboo might have made some attractive and distinctively Japanese fences, but, alas, there was only ham-fisted me to do the work here. After some time, I found a sketch of a fence in one of the books. It looked Japanese in style, if only by virtue of the cap on top and the decorative strips under the cap.

I couldn't use the design in the sketch as it stood as I was constrained by the neighbors' fences on both sides of it. When I measured across from the fence on the north to that on the south, I realized that they differed in height by more than two feet. But the cap would enable me to disguise the difference at both ends. Instead of the four-foot planks of the diagram, I decided—to be more coherent with my neighbors—to go with five feet. I measured up the space, calculated the amount of wood I would need, and bought rough cedar 4" × 4"s, 1" × 8" boards, miles of 1" × 1"s, and various other bits and pieces. I had to be away for a few days and so had it delivered. Bad move. The tarnished knights of the lumberyard have no interest in choosing the best pieces of wood for an anonymous order; indeed, they are eager to get rid of the junk that buyers would never select for themselves. So when the pile arrived, some of it was less than beautiful.

I set aside the damaged boards and took them back to the lumberyard to exchange. It is hard for the middle-class type to get lumberyard chic quite right. One can try to mimic the professionals, with worn and faded jeans, the battered and soil-encrusted tape measure clipped to the belt, the rugged shirt, and pencil stub behind the ear. A three-day beard helps. But it is the confident, contemptuous look I can't manage. At the other end of the scale is the guy who drives up in his Mercedes, with Gucci loafers, starched designer work shirt, and "gentleman's jeans" to buy some exotic hardwoods and teak dowels. No doubt building harpsichords as a hobby.

Somewhere betwixt and between, I stumbled into the yard with the unsatisfactory boards under my arm. Whatever I had gained by my carefully neutral sartorial preparations, I immediately lost by wearing wimpish hard fabric gloves to prevent splinters. A real man would no doubt rub his work-toughened hands along the boards instead of using sandpaper to smooth them.

But however inadequate I feel in lumberyards, I am always slightly intoxicated by the wonderful smell of the wood. The dominant flavor of the day was cedar.

A slim, red-haired young man came toward me. He glanced at the boards as he approached, open-mouthed, showing what seemed to be disproportionate horror at their condition even before I could begin to complain. He pointed at them as though to make them disappear. He seemed more distressed than I was. His long face and pale blue eyes displayed outrage that anyone would sell such stuff to a customer. "Rubbish! It's rubbish!" Had the boards been pointed, I felt he might have impaled himself, unable to deal with the shame. I began assuring him they really weren't so bad, apologizing for bringing some of them back. He helped me replace them with the very best he could find and slid the new boards into the trunk of my car with a delicacy that would have done a brain surgeon proud. As I pulled away, I saw him slide my returns back on top of the pile to await the next incautious customer. He had probably selected them for me in the first place. But he was a veritable Mozart of indignant sympathy.

I set about the fence.

First I rented one of those tools for digging neat holes for the supporting posts—a "posthole digger," it is reasonably called. It is like two narrow shovels hinged together. You drive them into the ground and pull apart the handles. This action forces the shovel-like blades to come together so that you can pull up and throw aside the first scoop of soil. In a surprisingly short time I was looking down into a three-foot-deep hole, not exactly elegant, but adequate.

By this point I found myself slowing down to watch the earth brought up by the digger. We walk across the surface, thinking little of what lies below our feet. Occasionally one sees massive excavations and the earth bared laterally. But this slow digging was disinterring a few inches at a time and showing with each small gift from the digger how varied were the layers of soil. The first few scoops were rich dark brown, decayed life, and then a dull russet more heavily laden with stones and with streaks of a richer red, and below that a grayer, heavy clay. I would become more closely familiar with these and other constituents of the three feet below the garden when digging out the pond.

One difference between the professional and the amateur is that the latter typically does each job only once and then moves on to another one-time job. The professional gets to make all the mistakes over the first half dozen tries at any job, and then learns the tricks and shortcuts and techniques. This project began to look as though it was going to be a series of hundreds of jobs, each of which would be done only once. I did have to dig three holes, and the third was discouragingly neater than the first. The neatness mattered, I was to discover soon, in that the first hacked and irregular one required a lot more concrete to fill around the post. I consoled myself that I would have to dig many more holes for the teahouse, so my small but accumulating posthole digging skill wouldn't go to waste.

Then I sweated away at mixing concrete in the new wheelbarrow. The pictures in the landscape design and construction book I bought are of calm men in immaculate clothing mixing the concrete with casual ease. I found it backbreaking and sweaty, and as it was the first time I had done it, full of anxiety. The trouble with mixing concrete is that you can't stop and think about it too much, or the stuff will set. I did the work with a spade, turning the dry powder over on the damp cement, then adding bits of water to get the right consistency—I hoped. I later read that one can mix the water and cement better with a hoe than a spade and thought I would try that when building the teahouse. When it seemed ready, I slurped the porridgy mess into the holes around the standing post.

It's hard to ignore the importance of this gray porridge mess to our civilization. Concrete isn't an immediately obvious candidate for heroic status, yet it provides the backbones and ribs and footings of our cities. Sand and gravel and cement and water, when they come together in the right proportions, hold much of our world in place. Joseph Aspdin, an English inventor, created Portland cement in 1824, and we have been using it in pretty much the same form ever since. It has immense strength, can be adapted to almost any form, and is fireproof, and there goes my last barrow-load around the final post. Rough, sloppy, and irregular, it will outlast every other part of the fence, to be carted away in twenty or fifty years' time, still in the shape of the holes I dug, clinging faithfully to the feet of the posts it is now settling around.

The result was three posts more or less vertical and more or less in line, in front of the shrubbery I was building the fence to withstand—at least for a little while. The principles of fence building are quite simple. First you establish thick upright posts firmly in the ground, usually by embedding them in concrete. Then you attach strips of slightly less substantial pieces of wood between the posts, one strip high up and the other close to the ground; these are called stringers. To these stringers you then attach the boards that constitute the most visible part of the fence. And that's it.

After a while I had the fence up.

In the photo of the fence you can see the mounding of the concrete that is desirable to ensure that the water flows away from the foot of the fence posts. The near post was my first effort, and I think I may have overdone it. But the rotten posts that had been hanging on to the old mesh fence I had removed were a vivid warning of the results of not keeping water away

The posts in place. Behind them is the riot of shrubbery the fence is supposed to keep at bay.

The fence in place, defending paradise.

from their feet. The original builder had put the mesh fence upright by nailing it to the posts; in the end the plant-tangled fence was the only thing keeping the rotted posts upright. No doubt that is a metaphor carrying a deep meaning for our lives, but I can't think just what it is at the moment.

One can get away with many small mistakes in building a fence, as the pieces in the end all stick together and hold one another up. The unignorable mistake I made, however, was using eight-foot spaces between the posts, and five-foot-long boards. The extra weight across the long bottom stringer encouraged sags like the dowager's pearls.

But getting this far had involved cutting and hammering cedar—one of the most aromatic and friendly of woods for building purposes. It is difficult to build anything without feeling affection for wood. Its utility to humans is so great that one could write the history of the rise and fall of civilizations in terms of the availability and exploitation of wood. Take the Roman Empire—well, someone did. Its power was built on the use of wood for much of its fortifications and for the great fleets that fed its cities from the grains of Egypt. The Empire's fall came with its inability to produce silver from its Spanish mines to pay the troops that held back the northern "barbarians." The silver required smelters, which were fueled with wood. As time went by, the forests that supplied the fuel were laid waste, and the costs of getting wood to the smelters proved excessive. So Rome couldn't pay its troops, so the barbarians overran the operation. Well, one's mind does tend to wander while thumping nails into wood, and admiring the material's hospitality in accepting the nails, and its willingness to grip and hold them for you. And don't take my analysis as the most reliable word on the Fall of the Roman Empire—I suspect someone has done a better job of accounting for it.

But I did have a problem with the thin strips of 1" × 1" wood under the decorative cap. The idea was to create the illusion that they extend through the posts. I cut the long pieces to fit exactly between the posts, and tacked them in place at both ends. This involved a fair amount of neck and arm bending; tacking small nails in the confined space under the cap wasn't wonderfully easy, and also involved a little more than the usual amount of hammering the occasional thumb and finger. But tacking the matching one-foot pieces onto the other side of the posts was much harder. The problem was in fixing such small pieces of wood firmly at a 90-degree angle. I found that after tapping in the first nail, the wood drooped down. After the second nail, it sloped off to the left. The third and fourth nails seemed unable to straighten it out, and after a while more metal than wood was evident. I tacked them more or less in place and decided to leave them to wait for inspiration, or the guidance of an expert.

A distinguished architect, who came to dinner one evening, a friend of a friend, seemed like the expert I had hoped for. I mentioned fences and problems with their building, and eventually insisted on showing him around the site. I pointed out my problem with the drooping strips. I had, until this desperation got the better of me, been wary of letting a professional see my efforts. I remembered the story of Sir Edwin Landseer Lutyens's comment on seeing Simla, the hill station in the Himalayan foothills (from which the British ruled India for much of the year, because they were unable to bear the heat of New Delhi): "If one was told that monkeys had built it, one could only say, 'What wonderful monkeys—they must be shot in case they do it again.'" I expected my architect friend to be less explicitly judgmental, and to come up with a solution to my sagging wood problem that involved some arcane technique that might need great skill or, more hopefully, some complex tool I might be able to rent. He looked sagely at the fence and asked if I had a source of very fine fishing line. "Tie it to the end of the hanging 1" by 1" and then staple the line to the inside of the cap above. No one will be able to see it." This reminded me of the similar tip an expert handyman decorator once offered when I asked how to fix a damaged wall tile in a bathroom. "Stick a picture over it." These pieces of advice seem to lack the Zen master touch.

Reflecting on the Zen master's likely approach as I stood worrying how to fix the droop, I recognized that the slender strips are a suggestion of frailty in the rough and hardy fence design. I have been fretting about how to make them firm and perfectly parallel, and so unlike anything human. I only slowly realized that their droop better characterized the human frailty our need for fences symbolizes. They want to droop, so let them droop. What had earlier seemed like a technical failure that caused me some small distress every time I looked at it, now has an unexpected charm. My slightly sloping strips oddly humanize the fence.

Ah, but does my decision to let the strips find their own

place in their own way owe more to Japanese principles of gardening and Zen insights or to an Irish readiness to accept a stopped job as a job finished?

The Japanese aesthetic, epitomized in the tea ceremony, aims for lack of symmetry and formal perfection. So we have the paradox that in the recognition of imperfection, one can engage in the process of perfecting. True beauty, in Taoist and Zen thought, can be discovered only by one who mentally completes the incomplete. "Completeness in every detail is undesirable," says Kazuko Okakura in *The Book of Tea* (1906; reprint, New York: Charles E. Tuttle, 1956).

Staining the fence

Having tested that the boards all fitted, I then removed them and began staining the fence supports on a fine sunny day. The sky clouded over early in the afternoon, and within a short time those ominous heavy-bellied purple-gray monsters were headed toward the fence. They drift through the sky effortlessly, but big clouds weigh thousands of tons, much of which they were preparing to drop on my fence. I knew that they had heard about the painting, picked up lakefuls of water, and were storming toward my garden intent on gleeful dousings. The instructions on the stain can laughingly informed me that unless the stain was kept dry for at least twenty-four hours, the work would be ruined. Sigh. Grabbing assorted bits of waterproof plastics from all over the house, including our daughter's tent tarp, I covered my handiwork.

Needless to say, it didn't rain.

For all the framing parts of the fence I chose a dark charcoal gray and then used a slightly dull, strong green for the boards. I had been looking at colors in Japanese gardening books, trying to fix on a typical or traditional matching set and, at one point, had imagined combining a rather pallid terra cotta with ocher. I had seen several buildings in shades of ocher, and thought it might go well with a kind of washed-out terra cotta. But I decided that the deep gray-black and green would present a more restful combination and even capture well one of the moods a Japanese garden might help one celebrate, that of melancholy. I haven't regretted my choice, but wonder whether it may be a little too much if I also use the same combination on the teahouse.

After finishing my fence, however, I read that one should never paint or stain a fence in a Japanese garden. One lets the wood weather naturally. The cedar would have become a satisfactory gray, complementing the natural greens of bamboo better than this green stain. What can I do? Too late to undo my sin. Story of my life, of course. Of all our lives.

There is something about handiwork that brings out in one's neighbors strange and unsuspected streaks of a curious form of sadism, disguised as advice or sympathy or as the passing along of helpful suggestions from their own experience. One man, whom I have never heard say a less than kind or cheerful word in twenty years, felt obliged to tell me stories of unimaginable disasters that inevitably resulted from using the kind of solid-color stain I had put on the fence. He had used it on a fence at his place on the island, and it had all peeled off in weeks. A friend of his had used it on a shed, and . . . well, I don't remember; maybe the thing fell down or imploded, killing all within. It seemed everyone in the city had used this stuff, without anyone learning from anyone else how useless it was. In some of the stories, it seems to have had effects that couldn't have been worse if concentrated nitric acid or a flamethrower had been deployed. I found constantly that friends or visitors—nearly always men who may themselves have had no experience building anything more than IKEA bookshelves—for some reason found great energy in enthusiastically, even rapturously, describing catastrophes that followed for someone they knew doing what I had just finished doing.

When the boards were in place, and I'd left them for a few days, it became clear that the bottom stringer could not support their weight. It became clear not just because one could see it, but because the boards in the midpoints between the posts, where the sag was deepest, fell out in a slight breeze. Even I knew that when the boards of one's fence drop onto the ground, something is not entirely right. The diagram I was following seemed to have weightless wood.

Providing support for the bottom stringer was essential. Several solutions came to mind, the first being approaches that would require the least work, like slamming a big stone under the midpoint of each eight-foot stretch. But, having wandered the neighborhood looking at how people prevented their fences from sagging (and earning suspicious looks as I pulled at grasses and poked around the base of various fences), I realized that the obvious cure was to screw another cedar 2" × 4" on its side under each of the sagging stringers.

I had decided, for some reason connected with their being in front of me in the hardware store, to try galvanized screws rather than nails for fixing the stringers to the posts. This proved to be a good decision. A screw has six times the holding strength of a nail the same size. Using two drills also saved a lot of time. I fixed a bit somewhat thinner than the circumference of the screw in one drill, and a screw bit that fitted the head in the other. Dragging the two gunlike drills along behind me, I easily made a guide hole with the first, then put the screw in place and zoomed it firmly in with the other. A dear friend who had died left the second drill to me a while ago, and somehow it was comforting to use her tools on this slightly mad project, as though she was still around taking part in the work. It was the kind of project she would have enjoyed, serendipitous and with the challenge of building without much of a preordained plan.

Drilling upward at about ground level, I had to brace myself by lying stretched along the trench I had dug the length of the fence. The dirt was satisfactorily dirty and no doubt added to the workmanlike authenticity of my jeans. One of our sons came out as I was putting the last screws in and was clearly impressed at the old man slogging through the muck, swinging from drill to drill like a mechanized gunslinger.

With the new 2" × 4"s under the center of the base stringers, the sagging problem was solved. The great feature of this kind of work is, as the French say: *Pas de probleme sans solution* (there's no problem without a solution). To create a convincing barrier against even the most malevolent of the neighboring weeds, I also dug a further six inches under the base stringer and wedged in place some black plastic lawn edging. I slotted it snugly against the 2" × 4", and packed the soil back around it on both sides. Nothing short of a three-headed titanium drill for an oil well could get through now, I foolishly thought—not recognizing that the tender shoots of bindweed are more powerful than our most massively abrasive machines.

The japonica quince

Among the overgrown shrubs, the bindweed, the blackberry, weeds, and ivy next door was a japonica quince. I wanted to preserve the quince from my devastation of everything else along the fence line. I also feared that if the lot was sold and someone got in a landscape gardener, as is common, and they started by razing the lot, which is also common, the quince would be uprooted with everything else. When the neighbors were back for one of their periodic cleanups, I asked whether I might "liberate" the quince, and plant it on my side of the fence. Shirley, the neighbor, said yes, but warned me that moving it would not be easy.

It was early summer, and probably not the ideal time to try to move the quince, but the lot might sell at any time and I could lose it entirely. And how hard could it be to move a bush, even a tall one? I began slicing around the base, some distance from the multiple stems. This was to be like the work of a brain surgeon, delicate and slowly persistent. Delicate and slowly persistent got a fair amount of soil moved, but made no impression at all on the rootedness of the quince. To make matters worse, its roots had cleverly matted themselves around some fair-sized rocks. I was clearing some serious space but, even though some of the stems began to move like loose teeth, the whole plant gripped the earth with admirable and infuriating tenacity.

By this time I was sweating, thirsty, and hungry. I had also dug a splendid hole for the damn thing on my side of the fence, which it could see if only it looked. I had even packed the hole with dark soil from my compost heap to welcome it. Yet the roots seemed to go down forever. I wanted to avoid cutting them, but couldn't get much further down and around the bowl of the roots, due to stones, to the roots themselves, and to the mess of other plants around. I had been patient, and persistent, and delicate. And then I got the mattock.

After a few swings, it became clear why brain surgeons don't much use mattocks in their work. A deep sideways slice cut under a part of the bush, severing the roots, and about half of it flopped over. It still had a fair amount of root attached, but the rest of the tall bush just stood there. Pulling carefully, then not at all carefully, I couldn't dislodge the still-standing stems, so I piled composted soil around them, and filled the hole, leaving the better-rooted half of the quince where it was. The liberated half I carried across the line to the prepared hole, dug it in, and then watered both sides profusely. With any luck, next spring I would have japonica quince flowers on both sides of the fence. As the summer passed, the old rooted half of the tree in the neighbor's yard drooped a little, then picked up and looked quite cheerful. The half on my side drooped, and drooped some more, and dispiritedly let its shriveled leaves fall. Soon they were entirely gone, and I was to spend the summer trimming it back and watering the bare forked sticks with faint hope.

Beginning the wall

When I had begun the fence, digging out soil to make holes for the posts and digging away the top covering of grass, moss, and weeds of one kind and another, I had tossed my spadefuls behind me where I assumed the raised garden would be. The weeds, stones, and soil would serve as its base. But the increasingly untidy mound needed shaping and constraining. If water from a pond was to be pumped to the top of the garden and run through it in a short stream, I would need to build a wall to support the back and sides of the raised garden.

I would, in the centuries to come, need to be able to back a lawnmower out of the shed behind the intended garden. So I pulled out the lawnmower from the shed, stood behind it, pushed and pulled it a bit, and noted the approximate amount of space needed to maneuver it. Then, after consulting books about building walls and incredulously admiring the immaculate workers in the photographs, I dug a line about a foot wide parallel to the shed and compost heap. At the east end, I curved it around to run parallel to the fence, about three feet away from it. At the west end I curved it across the lawn where the playhouse had stood, stopping at roughly the point I assumed the pond would be. I dug down about eight inches or so and filled the small trough with compactible gravel.

On my way home from work the next day, I stopped at a landscape supply center to choose stone for the wall. There are acres of almost every kind of stone one could imagine. It is a lapidary paradise (though Western iconography has Paradise somewhat short of stones, relying more on fluffy clouds and perfect lawns for its landscape supplies, whereas the other place seems to be mounded with boulders, usually smoldering). Once past the gate, there are shoulder-high mounds of stones, bound in wire and tough plastic. Farther back they tower higher, as pallets are piled one on top of the other. The first sets are wall stones, from gray basalt, through endless shades of green and brown, to rose and ocher, and pretty well any color you might want. Nature seems to supply them all. I parked the car and ambled among the mounds, delighting in their names and textures. Here's a dark pile of "midnight slate," and, next to it, "tumbled Pennsylvania bluestone," followed by "Kootenay jade," "green marble," and "mountain blueberry." On the other side is "random summer sunset slate," "Kootenay rainbow rock," "goldleaf," "Mile 40 river rock," and "Bristol Isle river flats." (No one at the yard knew where Bristol Isle is. There is a tiny Bristol Island out in the south Atlantic, I discovered, but that hardly seems a likely source of the stones. The guys I talked to assume they are from somewhere in British Columbia. More research is needed.)

I decided on the gray basalt and ordered four tons. The yard manager, a slim, laconic man, assured me they would arrive the following afternoon at 2 P.M. Exactly to the minute, the truck backed into our driveway. The heavy driver lowered himself carefully from his cab and climbed onto the rear, where he fastened the hook of a small crane onto the first pallet of stones.

I asked him whether he minded my taking some pictures of his delivery. Climbing up into the cockpit, he managed a small sigh, looking a bit contemptuously at my common old camera, and said, "Sure," somewhat like a reluctant superstar granting a favor to a teenage fan. He let me know that his unloading operations were usually videotaped, and that he had probably starred in more films and photographs than had most movie actors.

As I clicked away with the Minolta, he slowly lifted the pallets of gently swaying stones and lowered them onto our blacktop. He drove away, leaving me the small job of wheelbarrowing the four tons to the rear of the garden.

Delivery of the wall, in pieces.

Building the wall was both easier and harder than I had expected. The easier part was laying the first layer of wide stones onto the compactable gravel, and then laying a second layer on top of them, and a third layer on top of them. Whatever irreg-

The beginning of the wall for the raised garden.

ularities led to misfits and wobbliness between the first and
second layers were solved by the third layer. The enormous
weight of these long, flat stones crushed the lower layers into
firm bases for yet a further layer. Once I was up to layers five
and six, the first layers were immovably solid. I sloped the stones
inward toward the space where the garden would rise. Sloping
each layer of stones a few inches further inward than the one
below it added to their ability to support the soil, which, when
heavy with rain, would need a lot of weight to contain it. The
wall was to serve like ten strong men, pushing back against the
soil, holding it in place. I then threw the mound of soil against
the rising stone wall, stomping the soil hard against the stones.
The landscaping fabric that I put on the inside of the wall would

prevent particularly adventurous weeds from finding a way out through the chinks between the stones.

The harder part was making the inward slope of the wall regular. Occasionally, I overdid the slope a bit, then would overcompensate. The result is something less than perfect, but at this point starting again was something my back and knees would not hear of. This stuttering irregularity is the character it will have to live with. I continued around the curves at fence and garden sides, but ran out of stones. I would need more basalt, but for now I had a semicircle of wall into which I could toss any further soil, and when the time came, I also could mound the deposits from the excavation for the pond.

The black bamboo and its water barrier

I imagined a strip of about three feet in front of the fence with a few patches of bamboo, growing through a covering of small stones. Why does one develop enthusiasms about things one knows nothing much about? Descriptions of black bamboo's ebony stems and rich green leaves made it sound romantically ideal. I should have attended a little more to what the books might have meant in calling it an "aggressive running variety." I faced two problems: first, finding some, and second, constraining it from taking over the city.

Bamboo, a grass, is one of the more distinctive and mysterious plants. It is a part of the fabric of the history, culture, and practical daily life of China and Japan, though the word "bamboo" is Malayan. Black bamboo grows to about twenty feet, and bends gracefully and flexibly in rain and under snow, moving constantly in the slightest breeze. It will be ideal for softening the lines of the fence and harmonizing with the greenery of the trees beyond. To disturb the starkness, symmetry, and regularity of the fence, I wanted to put in three bunches of the bamboo, irregularly spaced, and irregularly distant from one another.

Some bamboos grow to more than a hundred feet, and create magical forests with little undergrowth, more like the interior of an alien but civilized house than a wild place. Su Tung-P'o, a Sung-dynasty poet of the eleventh century, wrote:

> There are bamboos
> ten thousand meters high
> if you look at their shadows by moonlight.

The main problem with black bamboo is its slight tendency to "run" rapidly and everywhere over the planet. Containment requires digging down about three feet, and then putting in a "water barrier"—concrete or a tough, flexible, impermeable plastic. I tried nurseries in vain looking for water barrier material, until I was directed to the one place in town that dealt in trees and everything to do with them. A soft-spoken young woman at a small nursery near our house gave the directions. She spoke so softly that I had to crane closer to hear. I was there because I had been phoning around looking for black bamboo, and she had whispered the news that they had just received three tubs of it. I bought them immediately, and was then ready to equip myself to constrain their rambling tendencies, so set off for the tree place.

It had been raining and stopped just before I arrived. I stepped carefully through the mud-riddled yard, avoiding pools and streamlets, and ducking past massive machinery. The place was macho and surly beyond the muscled fantasies of the lumberyards. I passed tattooed and hairy guys who chewed trees for breakfast; they were pulling huge chains off spools and slinging cables in the backs of pickups. They disdained to look at anyone not dripping oil and mud. I entered the shop through a side door from a huge covered storage and service area, where some long-haired and even more muscled mechanics were clanging on a huge-wheeled tractor.

The shop did little to change the ultramacho impression of the tree-fixing business. Most of what I could see piled on the floor and hanging randomly from walls looked like a sideline in Hell's Angel's armaments, designed for murdering trees rather than doing them good. The floor was of broad dusty boards that could have graced Dawson City in the gold rush days.

"I'll be down in a moment!" A woman's muffled voice came from above, German accented. It seemed unlikely she would have heard me over the cacophony from the service area outside. Perhaps she could see me through the cracks between the planks that formed the floor above. I anticipated a Teutonic wrestler, sporting as much facial hair as some of the guys outside.

Down the wooden stairs came the unmistakable click of high heels, and smiling a welcome was a young blond woman wearing an ensemble right out of one of those luxurious fashion magazines: a light purple sweater—cashmere it looked like—with a neat skirt and, I swear, a string of pearls.

What could she help me with? I described my desire to have three patches of black bamboo and my desire not to have them take off at a gallop across the neighborhood. Water barrier! She seemed disproportionately delighted, as though I was a valued ally in the battle against uncontrolled bamboo. It came five feet in width, of any length I wished.

"I want to have three sets, about three feet long on average and maybe a foot and a half wide."

"So, three feet and six feet is nine feet each one. By three. You should buy fifty feet. You always need more."

She walked behind the plywood facing that blocked off the stairs, and came back a moment later wrestling with a mighty roll of deeply gleaming black plastic. Another woman came into the shop behind me.

"Can I help?" I asked.

"No, no. I can manage." I thought I shouldn't push the

macho stuff in this setting, though the roll seemed not only to be awkward, slippery, and heavy, but also to have a will of its own.

"Jane, come and help." Presumably the Jane who had just entered was not a customer. As I looked around, she took off her coat and dropped it on the handle of what I was later to learn was that miraculous tool, a come-along. Jane seemed to be a schoolgirl, or perhaps a college student, with the lank and unkempt hair of the guys outside, and was wearing jeans and a sweater quite unlike her friend's.

Jane held one end of the strong black plastic while Cashmere and Pearls began to unroll it. It was very stiff and unwilling to come off its roll without a struggle. As Cashmere hugged and pulled the bulky roll, Jane found herself dragged sideways by the coiled force of the plastic. As they unwrapped it, they had little room to work in, and each of them was bracing against the counter or the plywood wall. Within minutes it seemed clear they were in a battle they weren't going to win easily. With about three feet unrolled, Jane was pulled forward and just stopped herself from falling, but her force toppled the precariously balanced roll till it thudded against the counter, Cashmere and Pearls hugging it and trying to pull it back.

They started with a few shouts of surprise and outrage, which became splutters of giggling. Jane tried to help by pulling against her end, but went over into it, falling and pushing the plastic over with her. This helped spring the roll away from the counter in Cashmere's embrace, and she went down, sprawled not entirely gracefully astride it. Both women tried to haul themselves up, hindered by the uncooperative plastic. They absolutely refused to accept any help and were by this point in tears of laughter at their ungainly struggle.

After some brutal minutes, in which the battle could have gone either way, they managed to work out a technique whereby Jane backed toward the come-along, pulling and dragging from side to side, while Cashmere wobbled the roll as she turned it, her pearls all the while clicking against the plastic. Once Jane had retreated to near the rear wall, Cashmere began measuring, and put a piece of masking tape at the twenty-foot mark. Things became a bit nasty again, as Jane had now to roll up her end while they simultaneously were trying to unwind it from the other end. By this time, laughter was seriously handicapping both women. But with heroic efforts, they managed somehow to get fifty feet from the tight bale and roll it up in a carryable bundle. Cashmere and Pearls took up a utility cutter and sliced the roll from top to bottom with a deft wrist and the practiced ease of an Argentinean knife fighter.

I paid, thanked them heartily, and strode out into the yard with the water barrier under my arm. As I tiptoed my way back across the muddy yard's pools and streams, various of the tattooed and oiled workers nodded and smiled, a few called out "Good afternoon," and one wished me luck with the water barrier. Perhaps I had been the surly one going in, and the happier man who came out elicited a happier response.

Back in my garden with the impressively black water barrier—it had that deep, numinous, utter blackness of the slab in *2001*—I was now ready to get the bamboo into the ground. First I had to dig holes for it, about three feet down, two feet wide, and five feet long. The soil in this area clearly generates stones. They are born as tiny pebbles and grow rapidly in the ground like potatoes, only without any genetic program to control their development. The frustration of constantly having to dig out stones was alleviated a little by realizing they would come in handy for the garden.

As the day wore on, I wondered whether any of the neighbors might be peering through curtains to see what I was up to. These holes looked suspiciously like graves. Perhaps they might be watching to see whether I would later drag cumbersome sacks dripping blood over the lawn. I dug down three

The gravelike water-barriered holes for the black bamboo.

feet or so, then measured and cut the black water barrier. My clumsy slicing led me to appreciate the skill of Cashmere and Pearls. Everyone had told me how the bamboo would escape from the barrier if I left even a tiny gap, so I overlapped the two ends and stuck them together on both the inside and outside with double-sided, waterproof carpet tape. I slotted the roll of plastic into the grave, dumped back some of the soil I had just dug out, planted the bamboo, and filled around it with the rest of the soil. I had been told that bamboo is happy with poor soil, which seemed a bit unlikely, so I gave each stand a few full spadefuls from the compost heap.

Once the three sets of bamboo were in place, I covered the strip in front of the fence with landscape fabric to discourage weeds coming through. This material was new to me, as I'd never done any gardening except for growing vegetables. The black mesh fabric seemed like cheating. But any ally against weeds is to be welcomed. I left uncovered the areas inside the water barriers around the bamboo, so they wouldn't have a problem sending up new shoots. Not that the bamboo would have the problem—it would come through almost anything—but it might push up the fabric and disrupt the gravel and stones, generally making a mess.

The next preemptive strike against weeds was a generous layer of compactible gravel. Before spreading the gravel, I dug a narrow trench with the spade and wedged in some of that plastic lawn edging, to hold the gravel in place.

After covering the strip with gravel, I replaced the fence boards, which I had removed when reinforcing the stringers. As I put them between the stringers, I realized that it always surprises me when things I have carefully measured actually fit together properly when it is time to assemble them.

The three sets of bamboo were of varying height and bushiness. In the rain they gracefully bow and rise again. In the snow of the following winter they gathered flakes and leaned

The stained fence, the quince, and the sets of bamboo. It's pretty good so far, despite the uprights being a bit off and the slight sags here and there (perfection would challenge the gods). But a border for paradise is in place. The wilting and much-cut-back japonica quince is in the right foreground.

over with them to the ground. I would tap them gently to release the snow, and the stems would slowly ease themselves upright, apparently grateful but no doubt quite indifferent. I had come to delight in their rich sharp leaves, so distinctive and elegant. The care of plants is of particular concern in the Japanese tradition, especially in monastery gardens, where the monks apply ultimate solicitousness. In Kazuko Okakura's *The Book of Tea,* the author suggests that each plant should have a special attendant to care for its needs. Some might need their leaves washed with soft brushes made of rabbit fur, and "It has been written that the peony should be bathed by a handsome

Testing different colored stones against the fence.

maiden in full costume, that a winter-plum should be watered by a pale, slender monk."

My final task here was choosing the stones to cover the strip around the bamboo and quince. While the plastic edging I had slotted in to keep the gravel in place created a sharp straight line, the stones of the pond and its curving wall eventually would cover and hide that line. Avoiding such lines is important because, in Japanese mythology, devils can walk only in straight lines; this is why zigzag paths and curves are an integral part of any Japanese garden. So the mythology supports an aesthetic principle, and the realized aesthetic principle playfully reflects the mythology. I found some bluish-gray pebbles in the stonemason's yard that become nearly black when wet. They have an undramatic, dignified appearance. I was tempted also by some dull purple stones that became variedly dramatic when wet. They went well with the green but reminded me too much of the colors of just about every restaurant and public building of the past few years. Lavender and green seem to have been every designer's favorite combination. I did find a use for them later, though, when building the path behind the wall of the raised garden.

With this impregnable fence in place to keep anarchic nature on the other side, I set about digging out the pond, adding to the dry-stone wall that would contain the raised garden, paving the area behind the first stretch of wall, and so on. From each of these tasks I would occasionally look over at the fence, thinking that my floral foes were securely kept at bay. But within weeks I saw tendrils of green creeping across the crushed gravel, and even racing toward the bamboo! I couldn't believe it. The bindweed had plainly spent the intervening weeks looking for tiny gaps and squeezing itself in. Why? It had a totally free range next door, and could spread where it wanted. Why was it spending its time and ingenuity looking for chinks in my fence? And this was no doubt just the beginning. I had impulses I shouldn't confess to in a book about gardening—connected with a foray next door armed with a flamethrower and a Schwarzenegger enthusiasm for using it.

And then, after a few more weeks during which I took some small pride in how well the bamboo had settled, I saw the leaping rhizomes. I have been slow to realize that gardening is war carried on by other means, the most ancient war which we languaged animals have fought against nature. Here I had gone to the trouble of digging in my smooth and flawlessly black industrial water barrier, leaving it poke a couple of inches above the crushed gravel so that it might be level with the layer of stones still to come, and what is the bamboo trying to do within weeks of being given the hospitality of my paradise to be? Not content with extending its underground shoots around what seems to me an entirely adequate space, it is sending the rhizomes up into the air, trying to leap over its edge and dive into the ground on the outside. At least, that's what I assumed until I later learned that these were not rhizomes but rather tired late culms poking up then falling over sideways, exhausted at the prospect of going up another dozen feet or so. I went round with the pruning shears and clipped the bent culms back. But I began to feel that I might have taken on a battle with a far hardier warrior than I could begin to imagine. If this is what they are getting up to where I can see them, what is going on underground? Perhaps the three-foot depth to which I sank the water barrier is laughable to these wildly proliferating giant grasses.

Mentioning bamboo is to invite horror stories. *The Day of the Triffids* is nothing compared with some of the stories I have been told, of unstoppable bamboo whose root mass was the size of a house, going down twenty feet; of the invasion of a neighboring yard and, before anyone knew, the bamboo had grown through the swimming pool, costing $15,000 to fix; of legal entanglements and eternal bitterness between neighbors; and of endless, hopeless attempts to control clumping forests of the stuff. Perhaps I will be able to add my catastrophe in a while.

But the fence was up, protecting paradise, and so it was time to get on with building the paradise the fence was to protect. Paradises need running water and ponds for it to fall into, so time to put that ancient and wonderful tool, the spade, to serious work.

Building the pond

THE IDEA WAS THAT THE soil I dug out for the pond would become the raised garden. And the height of the raised garden would be determined by the amount of soil dug out. Two problems quickly became apparent, and a few thousand others emerged as the project went forward. The first problem was with the topsoil — compounded from millennia of flesh, fur, and feces, as T. S. Eliot so nicely put it — in addition to millennia of trees, underbrush, and light green spongy bog plants in this rainforest climate. I spaded out the rich brown soil and threw it against the first bit of the wall of the to-be-raised garden. As I dug down, I tossed out a lower layer of attractive red-gold-yellow sandy soil, and then, from deeper still, heavy gray clay, both of which went on top of the good soil. Ideally, I would have lifted the whole lot out in one scoop and deposited it right way up for the garden, with the topsoil on the surface.

I began to try to remedy the problem as I extended the hole, by tossing the topsoil to the left and the sandy soil and clay to the right. The idea was that I would somehow get the good soil on top of the clay when I started moving it around for the garden. I'm not sure how I imagined I was going to slide the clay under the topsoil on the left. But once I dug the soil out and deposited it on what was to be the raised garden, it seemed to expand in some mysterious way. After a while I had a decent-sized hole in the ground but an indecent amount of soil on the garden. "Raised" began to look like a joke; sky-garden seemed more appropriate. Any waterfall from this height would probably stun the fish. I assumed I would have to get someone in to cart off most of the clay. But the last mini-mountain was all clay, and my plan to deposit the good soil to the left began to seem silly as I was covering the whole area five or six feet deep. I could have made the pond smaller of course, but I had a responsibility to give the fish a decent chunk of real estate to do their fishy things in.

This was one of the activities in which first reading a book or two about digging out ponds might have helped. When I later found some in the library, I saw that they all begin with the sensible suggestion that one should first plan precisely the area of the pond, marking it with a hose or something equally flexible that one can lay on the unsuspecting ground. I had just begun digging in what seemed roughly the middle of the intended pond and then enlarged it into a shape that seemed pleasing. The books also recommend that one lay out two large tarpaulins. Onto the first one tosses the topsoil, which one excavates completely; then, when digging out the clay, one tosses that onto the other tarpaulin.

Easy.

Too late.

Stones are perhaps the first necessity for a Japanese garden, but the second is water. We can so easily project our emotions into the movements of water. It can rage and lie silent, can be rippled by small or strong winds, can seem leaden and slug-gish or light and joyful. A body of water offers endlessly vary-ing mirrors of the world above it. Still water can reflect the moon, can dissolve it when a fish jumps or a pebble is thrown, and then reassemble it again from the withdrawing ripples on the surface. It doubles the green of plants, and mysteriously increases light while casting a darkened reflection of the world above. As it moves, it creates a kind of music ideally tuned to the human soul, whether the movement is its lapping against rocks or running over stones and falling into a pond.

The vague image that was guiding my digging was of quite a largish pond, given the space I had to work in—about fourteen feet by nine would fit nicely, I thought. I imagined a low stone wall around its rim, and a stream with perhaps three waterfalls, that need pose no threat to Niagara, dribbling through the raised garden among evergreen plants. But even as I dug I knew that realizing this ideal would involve a nefarious and shameful case of dendricide, or tree murder.

The problem was the birch tree that grew from the condominium garden, a corner of which backed up to ours. The birch forked in two at about head height, one fork leaning entirely over where the pond was to go. Its trunk had also burst through the old fence put up close against it when the condominium was built, by people who must have assumed the tree would stop growing in admiration of their fence. The expanded tree, which had muscled its way through the fence boards as if they weren't there, made it impossible for me to extend my new Japanese-style fence. This birch was a dirty old tree, oozing gallons of heavy, sticky sap in the spring, using the hint of a breeze as an excuse for flinging down bits of twigs throughout the year, and depositing its considerable wealth of undistinguished leaves in the fall. There was no point putting in a pond while this loomed over the area it was to occupy. I had the legal right to take out the fork that took a semi-corkscrew twist over the fence to trespass in my garden. Removing that whole fork, though, seemed likely to kill the tree, so I assumed I should try to negotiate with the condominium people to take out the whole thing. I was prepared to pay for it if necessary, but hoped I might do a deal whereby they would pay half. The only possible ground for them feeling any obligation at all was that the trunk was breaking down their own fence.

A little warily, I went round one afternoon and knocked on the door of Mr. O'Reardon, the chair of the tenants' council of the condominium. He, a little warily, began to amass his negotiating arguments as soon as he heard my request. His opening gambit was to tell me regretfully that they had already spent their budget for landscaping for the year. (This was May.) But he would come and see the problem. On the way we established that we had been born not far from each other in Ireland, and things were looking decidedly better by the time we reached the offending birch. He peered over the fence, and immediately agreed that he was witnessing an unforgivable trespass by the birch tree. And something must be done. He would put my request to the tenants' committee and would be back in touch with me.

The digging went well for a while, apart from the alarming expansion of the soil once it came above ground. Digging feels like fulfillment of one of our basic instincts—well, perhaps a little up the scale from basic—and such fulfillments are always pleasurable. Digging deeper and deeper, I worried that I might be unable to rein in my instinct before plunging to Grand Canyon depths. Most of the books suggested that a couple of feet would be enough, but I was approaching three and still going happily.

Perhaps it's the Irish genes, but I do greatly enjoy moving earth around. It is such miraculous stuff, infinitely fertile. In an average gram of soil, 10,000 different species of microorganisms live, socialize, reflect on their unimpressive lot, and die. There is greater biodiversity in each gram of soil than in all the mammals of the world. I'm not sure that reflecting on this as one walks across the lawn is likely to enhance one's confidence during an average day. And soil has the strange ability to make itself at home wherever one throws it; within days it looks as though it had been there since the beginning of time. The joy of digging kept me cheerfully descending inch by inch into the earth. Those endorphins kicking in, perhaps.

I am reminded that on a recent visit to Hong Kong, a Welsh colleague talked eloquently to our Chinese host about the pleasure-releasing effects of endorphins in the brain, making difficult learning its own reward. Our host listened attentively for some time, and then diffidently asked, "Ah, about the dolphins . . . ?" This was followed by the Welshman discussing the importance of eloquence as a much-neglected aim of education these days. Again our host listened intelligently and politely, after a while asking only, "Ah, about the elephants . . . ?"

A couple of the books said that the deeper the pond, the less likely it was that it would become murky with algae, and also that the fish would have a happier time, especially in the winter.

Moby Rock

Childhood stories lay down expectations the adult mind can't entirely escape, and each chink against a stone for a millisecond sparked images of pirates' casks, whose gleaming gold doubloons and heavy strings of opulent pearls might just about pay for this extravagance. Then I hit the rock. I already had hit many rocks, and I kept digging around this one to lever it out with the shovel. But it soon announced its boulder dimensions.

I dug and dug, and couldn't find a limit to it. Also, it seemed to be lodged in hard gray clay that resisted the tip of the shovel, reluctantly releasing an eggcupful at a time. Soon I was approaching five feet down around the stone. I had been thinking I was in *Treasure Island*, but it was turning out to be *Moby Dick*.

I gave up digging around Moby Rock after an hour or so, and after a further couple of hours on the next few days. A

Moby Rock emerges after twelve thousand years.

number of people looked at it; the electrician whom I had asked what I would need to do to get the teahouse and pond pump ready for his ministrations, the gardener who came to look at a tree that was diseased (suspiciously after his pruning of it), and various friends. I announced that I thought I would put soil back around the boulder and lay the liner over it. No, no! They were unanimous that it must come out. Think how magnificent the stone would look on the garden! And then they would wave and go away. All giving more or less fanciful suggestions for how I could get it out. Mattock and spade, and sore back and knees, finally released the rock from the long embrace of the clay. How long had it been there, held in that clay embrace? The last Ice Age—twelve thousand years? I must ask an expert.

Moby Rock became an obsession. How was I to get it out? I tried levering it with 2" × 4"s, but they cracked before it gave the slightest hint it might even consider moving. When persuaded by a long metal bar to move an inch, and no more than an inch though I grunted and threatened to tear muscles, it settled back as soon as the bar was removed. Should I build a pulley over the excavation and hoist it out? One neighbor finally suggested I needed a come-along. And indeed I did.

A come-along is basically a couple of metal cables with a lever joining them in the middle. You attach one cable to a tree, the other to the object you want to move, and, as you pull and release the lever, the cables draw the tree and object closer together. In the expectation that the tree won't move, the rock should be pulled out of the pond toward the tree. And damn me if that isn't just what happened.

Mind you, it didn't happen as quickly and easily as that. My friend Geoff came over with an enormous car jack, which looked like the original. He assured me that it was a good thirty years old and in its time had raised cars out of ditches; which cars, it emerged from the dramatic telling, Geoff had earlier

Joshua gives Moby Rock a cautious examination. His inspection,
at least, didn't lead to suggestions about what I should do with it.
He found the really interesting part was jumping off the edge of
the pond-to-be and being caught by his father or grandfather, and
then being hoisted up to leap in again—a habit we'll have to break
him of before the water goes in.

driven into the ditches. This is the same eloquent Welshman
whose academic discourses in Hong Kong had raised inquiries
about dolphins and elephants.

We attached the cables around the rock and around the tree
and I began to lever slowly. It wasn't easy pushing and pulling
the lever, but it wasn't very difficult either. The first few lev-
erings made the cables taut; then, after the next, Moby Rock
irritatedly shrugged a little; with another couple it reluctantly
began to shift; and after a few more it was complainingly
scraping itself out of its clay bed and rising onto the floor of

Moby Rock on the move.

the excavation. Geoff was behind it with the jack, taking pressure off the straining cables. If they slipped, they might come lashing back and take me for a ride into the apple trees, or remove my head. As I levered, the rock began to saunter across the bottom of the pond floor and hardly slowed to climb up the three-foot wall of the pond toward the lawn. Now that it was into its stride, I felt it might just wander on, out into the street, perhaps, and, sniffing the unfamiliar air, hitch a ride downtown. To see this monster scraping up the side of the pond as a result of my simple pulling and pushing was well nigh incredible. No wonder people make a fuss about the invention of the lever. Was it Galileo or Newton, or one of those people who knew a lot about how things moved, who said that with a good lever and fulcrum he could move the earth? I now know what he meant.

Moby Rock in its new resting place. Whatever I build will have to go around it.

BUILDING MY ZEN GARDEN

And then it came out, scoring a chunk of earth from the lip of the pond as it peeked over the edge of the lawn and inspected us. A pale chunk of granite. We dragged it a few feet further toward the raised garden, and let it rest. It seemed like a troll, stuck for thousands of years, finally taking a slow arthritic crawl and climb, and now needing a few more centuries to rest and catch its breath. We had a beer.

How long, I wondered, would it rest here? Another twelve thousand years seemed excessively optimistic. When we sell or die, the house will come down, a new one will appear, whose owner may not want a Japanese garden at the back, and away Moby Rock will be swept—perhaps back into the drained pond where it might feel more at home. When the neighbor's house to the north was crunched and carried away, the new owners wanted a new garden. A guy with a backhoe came in—he was a veritable Mozart of backhoers—and he set about flattening everything. At one point he hit a huge rock, bigger than Moby. He dealt with it in minutes; dragging it clear on the surface, then extending the backhoe feet and settling them firmly in place, he scooped out a capacious hole beside the rock, raised the bucket beside it, and tapped it gently into the hole. He filled in the hole, covering the rock, and leveled the soil all around in minutes. No doubt these rocks are weary and irritated at being disturbed at this hectic modern pace every century or so. So Moby Rock might be pushed around before it has a chance to sprout a decent coat of lichen or moss. I should help it along with a pasting of yogurt.

Preparing the pond
With Moby Rock now outside the hole looking in, I was able to continue with the pond excavation. I threw a considerable amount of clay into the hole left by the rock, leveling the base at about two and a half or three feet. That seemed enough.

Once the overall shape and depth seemed adequate, I began

Looking from the house at the excavation and excavator. The
teahouse is to go to the left of the hole that is to become the pond.

laying a long 2" × 4" piece of wood across the excavation,
trying to get it level. It was crucial to get it right, or the pond
would flood over and away at the lowest point of the rim. So
I shaved a sliver off this side and added one over there, patted
down a bit here, and took a slight chunk from that side.
When it was level all around the rim and level at the base, I
did some final sculpting of the sides, making the shelves
neater. Next I had to cover the surfaces of the pond—base,
sides, and shelves—with something that would protect the
vinyl liner from being punctured by a stone or sharp root
once the great weight of the water was in it. Being overly
cautious, I decided to put a layer of sand around first, and on
top of that to spread a layer of fiberglass insulation.

Slapping the wet sand on all surfaces proved hard on the back. The base of the pond was easy, as were the shelves, but the sides were sort of a pain. What am I talking about? It was agony. While that may be a slight overstatement, the damp sand had the terrible habit on this bright sunny day of drying out and dribbling down to the floor of the pond. More water onto the sand, and then slapping it back into place, evening it out, and in the end my sculpture of layers of brown earth became a somewhat more rounded one of uniform gray. I maybe put too much sand on the bottom, raising the depth of the pond to a bit over two feet.

Engaging in overkill, I then bought the thickest fiberglass insulation I could find and began laying it over the sand. The bright yellow strips looked vivid, but they also looked chunky. I couldn't make the footwide chunks fit neatly around the curves, but felt that the weight of the water would compress

Leveling the pond rim.

The earth sculpture for the pond, lined with damp sand.

them to a fraction of an inch or an inch. It was so difficult to cut the stuff to fit around the shelves that I decided I would settle for putting the battens of insulation on the base and sides of the pond below the level of the shelves, where the pressure of the water would be greatest. It looked dramatic, if a little daft.

Before doing the final work on shaping the pond, I had bought the liner. The landscape supply place had a section given over to ponds and liners, and examples of varying thickness. One of the books recommended at least 20 ml or even 30 ml thickness. This meant nothing to me. I described my project and the dimensions of the pond, and was advised to take the 40 ml liner. No doubt this helped their bottom line, but it seemed sensible, as the liner was no place to skimp.

The liner is made of polyvinyl chloride, hence PVC. In case

you know as little as I did about how such miraculous materials are made, I thought I should look it up. But after examining a number of sources, I'm not really ahead in the game of understanding. I gather that the liner is just one of the many forms PVC can be extruded into—if "extruded" is the right term—and is, as one of the books put it, "any of various tough, chemically resistant, thermoplastic polymers in which the repeating unit is $\cdot CH_2 \cdot CHCl \cdot$." This is how dictionaries and encyclopedias conspire to disguise the human meaning of such wonders as PVC. It is a product of astonishing human ingenuity, of individuals' dedication and insatiable inquiry, stretching back through the centuries as one curious person built on predecessors' findings, yet all this wonder and drama is suppressed. The understanding I was looking for was about who discovered what, in what circumstances, driven by what passions and hopes or fears. I know the information is somewhere in the library, but I'm afraid you are going to have to look it up for yourself. I have a pool to get on with, while gratefully acknowledging a debt to the unknown inventors of the miraculous PVC liner.

For a liner, one measures the length of the pond, adds its depth twice, and then one foot at each end for overlap, and then one does the same for its width at the widest point. Measuring generously and adding a bit at each measurement point, I reckoned I needed 22 feet long by 17 feet wide. It came in five-foot increments, so as I also needed spare liner for the stream, I asked for 30 feet by 20 feet. The guy who sold it to me was one of those who had got tough he-man chic to a refined, minimal art. I chatted about the project and what I thought I might need. He hardly spoke a word in response, grunted a couple of times, and did say, "I'll give you 40 ml. Good price." His only other words were:

"It'll be waiting for you over at the supply shed."

After I paid for it, I drove across the yard to avoid having to carry the liner all the way back to the car. In the huge open shed three guys were measuring and arguing. One began cutting, while passing judgment on the parentage and intellectual endowments of one of the others. This didn't fill me with cheer. As they walked across the black liner while cutting it, I felt much like a customer watching carpet salesmen clumping in big boots on a white Berber. They then began to fold it, and I realized I had another problem. It took the three of them to maneuver it, and even so these strong guys got it into the back of the car only with some difficulty. The rear of the car sagged under the weight. I asked whether they weren't planning to come and help me at the other end. They laughed, a tad dryly, as well they might.

Back home, I opened the trunk and looked at the heavy multifolded vinyl, wondering how I was going to get it out. My wife was at work, and our two strong sons and one strong daughter were away. I pulled the wheelbarrow up to the trunk and began heaving one side and then the other, pulling the top layer outward. I was able to unfold an inch here and then an inch or two on the other side. My strong wife came home as I was beginning to get the first layer over the lip of the trunk, and together we were able to pull more of it out toward the waiting barrow. Sweating (or glowing) and straining, we finally had a folded layer of the liner droop heavily onto the barrow, which shuddered. Once one chunk was over, we heaved at the next layer and gradually got it over the lip. Then, emboldened by real movement, we tugged the final chunk up and it reluctantly oozed out, hitting the barrow with a muffled thump that nearly had it over.

Buckle-kneed, I wheeled the barrow to the back of the garden, heaved the liner out onto the grass, and began to unfold it. Either I had been overly generous in my estimates, or the wrong guy had won the argument in the supply shed. It was the cutter's parentage and intellectual endowment that should have been brought into question. I could have covered a fair part of the neighborhood. No wonder it was so heavy. Without unfolding it all, I began to cut. It proved quite easy with a sturdy pair of scissors. With straining difficulty, I folded up the huge unneeded part and dragged it to the side of the lawn.

The books suggested that I should get a partner to help stretch the liner over the pond space, but as I set about the job the next day no one was home. I heaved the vinyl toward the pond, moving from side to side, gaining a few feet each time. Within half an hour I was covered with sweat, but the pond opening was covered with liner. Alas, instead of sagging into the space that was to be the pond, the liner sat unevenly on the fiberglass insulation battens. It had dragged them out of position on its way over, as the ice sheets had no doubt dragged Moby Rock.

There was nothing else for it but to fold back the liner as far as I could and struggle under it to pull the battens into place all the way around. This proved hopeless. It was like an antechamber to hell in there. The weight of the liner was considerable, and I had to hold it up with one hand while trying to locate a batten in the almost complete dark and pull it back to its proper place against the sandy side. As soon as I had a piece in place and untangled my sweating self from the humid world under the liner, the liner fell back and simply dragged the batten out of place again.

I spent some time futilely struggling to shove and hold the battens against the pond sides, till it became clear they were simply too big. I needed either to replace them with thinner and more maneuverable slices of insulation, or assume that the sand would provide adequate protection for the liner. The Irish assumption that all will be well if one takes the easier road won out. I sweated some more dragging the battens out, no doubt also scraping away some of the protective sand.

At this point my wife and daughter showed up, and I had

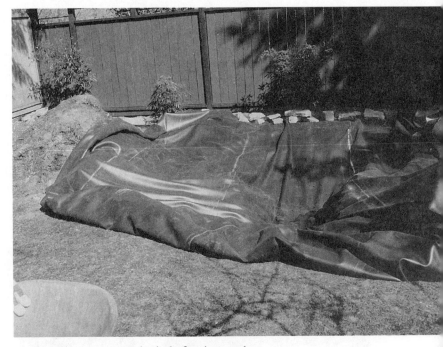

The liner hanging over the hole for the pond.

help fitting the liner into the pond, folding it over at the corners to minimize wrinkles. I laid just a few stones around the edges of the liner so that they would create some resistance when the weight of water pulled the liner downward into the pool. Once all was in place, we had the ceremonial squirting of water into the space to begin making it a pond.

Once the water was in, I cut away most of that vastly excessive load of liner. But I now needed more stone to build the small wall around the pond and finish the wall around the raised garden. By phone I ordered another three tons of basalt, and they promised delivery next day. Bang on the minute promised, the truck backed up the drive. The same driver as before climbed up to the cockpit of the crane at the rear of the truck and cautiously offloaded the stones onto our blacktop. He seemed a little puzzled that no one was taking photos or videoing him.

Here's Joshua, almost squirming with excitement. Just look at his fists. He was hopping from foot to foot. His aunt, Catherine, is holding the hose gun, and his grandma, Susanna, is ready to save him if he decides to dive in.

Filling up the liner.

I began the knee- and back-straining job of carrying this delivery of three more tons of stones from the driveway to the back of the garden.

Then it was jigsaw time. I began by laying the biggest and flattest stones around the rim of the pond, hanging them over as much as seemed safe so that they disguised or hid the liner. A stone at a time, and in a little while I had a pond with stones around it; after topping up the water and adding a few plants on the edge, it looked surprisingly like the real thing.

It seems as though it should be simple to set up a waterfall. But water has a peculiar habit of refusing to come over the stones one has set up. Instead, it inconveniently seeps behind them or beside them, with no appreciation of the aesthetic effect it might have if only it took the dive off the top stone and sparkled on the others as it tumbled musically down them.

Beginning to look like a pond. The water is to fall in on the right—just beyond the two small shrubs—if I can work out how to get it to flow properly over the stones. I had cut the liner away except where it was to provide a rear wall to the falling water.

Apart from that problem, I had to work out what the stream was going to be like and where it would flow. Initially I had imagined a pile of stone at the top rear of the garden—a ghostly echo out of time and place of those Chinese artists' abodes among mountains and rivers. Little they imagined, as they painted or wrote surrounded by silently padding servants and meltingly compliant concubines, of my struggles to emulate their physical surroundings in miniature. I thought I would lead the hose from the pump in the pond up to those top stones and the water would emerge into a small pool. It would then head down a winding stream with a couple of small waterfalls until it took the dive off the big stones into the pond.

While in a hardware store I saw a hard plastic minipond that I thought would be ideal for the top pool, so I bought it and lugged it home. It seemed to grow twofold in size when I put it on the raised garden. I keep forgetting just what a small space I am working in; it fills too big a place in my imagination. Still, I could surround the shaped plastic headpond with stones and ferns, and put a few water plants in it. But the need to keep the pond water clean undermined all this vague planning, which in turn led to a further unplanned building program. So the plastic minipond has remained a rather sad orphan, unused except for holding water plants in transition, watching the bog usurp its place.

The bog, the stream, and the waterfall

FOR FISH TO LIVE CHEER-
fully in a pond, the water must have certain qualities. A pond
owner, as I now suddenly was, has responsibilities to future
fishy tenants. A system was required that would clean the water
of waste from the fish, keep algae under control, and prevent
sludge and anything else undesirable from making its way into
the pond. It looked lovely and clear now, but despite my
meticulous early efforts, the time would soon come when all
kinds of detritus would be floating around and sinking down,
and algae drifting on easy breezes would dive eagerly into the
water and philoprogenitively multiply like crazy.

Having read about algae quickly transforming any pond, I
realized that that was all I knew about them, which seemed a
bit ungenerous, as we wouldn't be alive without them. There
are about 25,000 species of algae, from minute single-celled
creatures to leafy kelps more than 200 feet long. No part of
the earth's surface is free of them, from tropical jungles to the
Arctic tundra to downtown Philadelphia and to our backyard.
Algae carry out 90 percent of the photosynthesis on the
planet, and long ago they made the earth's atmosphere rich in

oxygen and thus hospitable to creatures like our ancestors, so I'll try not to complain too much when they make the pond opaque. They are the source of the food that ultimately sustains all aquatic life, including my goldfish-to-come.

The bog

The solution recommended in the books for keeping pond water sweet for fish is a biological filter that can deal with the microorganisms that play havoc with a pond and its life. The pump I had bought had a small "mechanical filter" on it—just a plastic grill to prevent the pump sucking up bits too big or hard for it to digest—but it did nothing for the water. The solution recommended in some of the more ambitious books was a biological filter bog. The company that made the pump also made a molded filter bog in three sizes. My pond would require the biggest. The water would be pumped along a flexible hose from the bottom of the pond into a connection on the plastic bog. This shot the water down to its base first, and the water then filtered up through layers of diminishingly sized stones, emerging at a lip that formed the beginning point of a stream that would carry the water back into the pond, cleaned. This looked very complicated, space consuming, and expensive. The size of bog I would need would run me more than $500. If people were willing to pay this for a piece of molded plastic with a few holes, it would be more prudent to invest in the company that made them than to buy its products.

Once again, what to do? I wandered around water garden shops. All offered those round filters with pads to put at the pump entrance. The pump sucks the water through the filter, drawing algae and muck and waste matter into it. At weekly or so intervals, it would be necessary to pull the whole thing up, unwrap the pad, swish it around in a pail of water to clean it, then fit the pad back around the filter, and lower the whole apparatus into the pond again. This seemed like a lot of nasty, slimy work. I want you to know that if that was what it took, I would do it, but I frittered away a few weeks looking around for less troublesome alternatives and asking questions in various shops. I had put a pile of oxygenating plants into the pond, so didn't mind taking a while as they helped the pond become more habitable for fish.

One trouble, and half relief, was that none of the filters I saw fitted my pump. But the company that made the pump, and the plastic bogs, also had a neat-looking set of filters that would slot easily onto the pump's intake opening. In the end, deciding I had to do something, I went to the landscape center where I had bought the pump and asked for some of those biological filters.

"They're useless," the sales clerk said, leaning on the counter with his arms spread wide as though ready to accept a fight about it. This seemed fairly uncompromising. A young, tall man, he had a curious manner of looking away while speaking, but not in the usual way of shifting to something close by and then back to the person with whom one is speaking. He gazed fixedly at something in a distant corner of the shop, as though he was watching it carefully. Then he would shift his gaze to something in an opposite corner, which also required his full attention. This was a tiny bit disconcerting.

"Well, what about those big filter bogs? Should I get one of those?" I had seen them hanging at the rear, hooked on the wall, with their soul-sapping prices attached. Perhaps the shop policy was to rubbish any cheaper solution and pressure innocent fish-loving customers to buy the plastic bogs.

"No. They're too expensive."

Well, we agreed about that.

"What should I do?"

"Buy some liner and make your own bog. Dig a hole, line it, and put layers of stones in, cover it with six inches of pea-gravel, just like you would have to in those fancy rigid bogs. There you are, for a tenth of the cost."

"Even less, as I've got a lot of liner left over from the pond."

"There you are." He nodded assertively at the decorative stones in the rear corner. "Those filters you attach to the pump are useless. You need a filter bog, and it will take care of itself once it's built. For a pond like yours"—he paused to stare critically at the light fixture—"you'll need to make it about four foot long by three foot wide and three foot deep. A good biological filter bog. That's the only way to go."

So that's the way I went. I left the place feeling quite cheerful at having saved a lot of money and a tad bemused that he wouldn't sell me either of the expensive items I would have bought. To compensate him, I bought my first water lily and a few heavy bags of pea-gravel. I also bought fifteen feet of "professional" hose, one inch in diameter, to carry the water from the pump at one end up to the bottom of the bog at the other, and a stainless steel clamp to attach the hose to the pump. But I also left feeling a bit daunted at the prospect of having to build a large bog. I had imagined that buying and sticking a filter on the pump would be enough. But the young man had convinced my conscience that I owed it to the fish to give them a proper filtering bog. Still, I went home quite encouraged. At last I had made a decision, and, after some weeks of shilly-shallying, could move forward.

Lowering the pump

First I decided to get the pump rigged up, with the black spiral hose attached, and then put it in place sitting on a couple of bricks at the deepest point of the pond. I cut an extra piece of liner on which to set the bricks, to protect the pond base. The efficient way of doing this would have been to climb into the pond and simply put them neatly one on top of the other. But the water was cold, and I really didn't want to climb in.

I think I also feared I might puncture the liner if I stood on a stone or something; in fact, I'm not sure why I seem to have concluded that I had to do everything from the sides of the pond. Perhaps it was a shortsighted method of avoiding one small inconvenience, while creating much greater ones I would have to deal with in the future. It may be tied to a suspicion that the world may end at any time; why go to trouble now for the sake of future conveniences that may never happen?

Anyway, instead of doing the straightforward thing and getting cold legs for a few minutes, I rigged up an unstable apparatus. The problem was how to lower the extra square of protective liner, with a couple of bricks on top of it, with a pump on top of them, and a hose attached to the pump, to the bottom of the pond. Bed was obviously the best place for dealing with these problems. So before slipping into sleep I lay visualizing how I might cut holes in the corners of the liner and run long pieces of string through each hole. The string would be doubled, so that once the three components rested on the bottom of the pond, I could release one end of the string at each corner and pull it out.

This operation, so smooth in my imagination, somehow ran into trouble with reality. My wife came home one day to find me proudly standing over the apparatus in the picture — so proudly that I took the picture. I persuaded her to take two of the strings, after I'd attached the hose to the pump, and I would take the other two, and we would stand on different sides of the pond and gradually lower the slipping, sliding, twitching apparatus to the bottom of the pond. She looked at the whole thing rather more skeptically and less admiringly than seemed to me appropriate. Even though it quickly became clear that she was right: the whole thing would stay steady only if we were holding it with exactly the same tension and lowering at exactly the same pace — which we couldn't manage. This teetering, tottering bundle, oddly

The pump on bricks on liner. The string is barely visible in the holes at each corner of the liner.

enough, against all reasonable expectations, did not dive sideways and disperse itself untidily around the floor of the pond. With wild jerks and much shouting from the two of us, the bundle settled itself according to the master plan, liner underneath, with the two bricks, and the pump sitting on the bricks. My wife was astonished, as was I—though I showed it less. We slid the strings out and marveled at Irish planning, with its excessive reliance on luck saving the day.

The pump is the heart of the system of circulation. Appropriately, it was after pumps were invented to clear medieval mines of water that William Harvey was able to work out for the first time the function of the heart in the human body.

Making the bog
I had plenty of liner left over, enough for the bog and stream, and for Lake Superior. I began digging at the high point of the garden, finding quickly that I would need to build a further wall on the pond side to support the bog. There was

enough stone left over from the rear and side walls. Taking up so much space with the bog also pretty well determined the shape of the rest of the raised garden, saving me, and humanity at large, from some of the designs I had been composing in my head. This bog, and the stream from it to the pond, would take up more than a third of the space available.

Digging and shaping the bog was familiar work; it was basically a small pond. Here I was able to do something for a second time, like the professionals. Pity I didn't do them the other way around, as I had learned a lot from my mistakes with the liner in the larger pond. The bog was a much neater affair—though no one would ever see it once the stones went in.

The digging went easily, as I was moving out soil that I had recently tossed here from the pond, and the lower foot or so I felt I recognized from the earlier excavation for the fence and bamboo. The more I learned, the more I looked at the soil with increasing respect. It takes, I had read, between 300 to 1,000 years to produce an inch and a bit of topsoil. So that's 10,000 years for the foot or so that is the minimum one needs to grow plants or crops. Adam came from a handful of Eden, and so ought to have been composed, as is most soil, of 50 percent oxygen, 33 percent silicon, 7 percent aluminum, 4 percent iron, and 2 percent carbon. Those 10,000 species of microorganism in each gram of soil are grateful that half of it is air and water, which they need to feed and reproduce. It doesn't look as though it can be much fun in there, but no doubt they see things differently.

What was I doing with this wonderful soil I was digging out? Well, there was nowhere on the garden to put it, so I shoveled it into the wheelbarrow and dumped it at the other side of the pond, in the space where the teahouse was to go. This is an Irish principle, of constantly moving things to wherever is immediately convenient, rather than thinking for a while and finding a long-term final place for them. Easier to

The excavation for the bog. The supporting wall is partly in place, and below it to the left are the stones surrounding the pond. The space between the pond and the bog will be a challenge later.

worry about that later. The principle at least keeps one moving on the job at hand, even if it creates unnecessary future work.

Once I was down about three feet and had shaped another attractive grave, I lined the base and sides with sand, folded the liner in place, and then faced a problem. How was I to get the flexible pipe from the pump to spread the water evenly around the base of the bog, and not be crushed by the stones I would be pouring on top of it? I laid an extra layer of liner on the base of the bog first, as added protection, and put the pipe in a circle over it. Then I drilled moderate-sized holes in the parts of the pipe that lay on the bog floor. I put bricks beside the pipe all the way around and laid large stones on top of the bricks. So I had the pipe circling like a tube in an underground railway tunnel. I thought this should ensure that

The bog with liner hanging out; a pom-pom juniper that I had planted earlier is behind it.

water would pour out more or less evenly around the base of the bog, and the stones wouldn't crush the pipe. I was quite proud of my cunning and only later realized that gravity would ensure that the water would rise uniformly, regardless of my circling and perforated pipe.

I then washed and carefully spaced a layer of large stones around the bottom of what was to be the bog. These were undistinguished stones that I had dug up in the process of building the fence and digging out the pond. But, as I increasingly came to see, one could not call any stone undistinguished. As time went on, I came to value the homely local stones most — though not enough to dig out the bog again to get at those I had buried.

I poured bags of drain-tile stones into the wheelbarrow, sprayed water over them, and rinsed them a couple of times to get the dust and clay off. Then I poured them in till they filled all the crannies around the first layer and were packed a foot or so deep. Next came a layer of still smaller stones— those round, tan-colored things people use in hydroponic gardening, which I hoped would be okay—and last came the pea-gravel. The job hadn't been as hard as I'd expected, and, lo, I had myself a biological filter bog. The only small remaining detail was to discover if it would work.

The books I had looked at while building the bog had diagrams of bog surfaces with small plants growing on them. The six or so square feet of watery gravel wouldn't be an attractive feature of the garden, but I didn't know what would grow in wet gravel. Any plant in its right mind would like some rich soil. But then I discovered there are odd plants that just love watery gravel, one of which is the water hyacinth. I bought a plastic bagful at a local nursery and tossed some onto the pond to float about and propagate. Then I pushed one hand down into the gravel to create space for each hyacinth's roots, set them carefully in, and smoothed the gravel around them.

One part of the fun of this project is the ramifying discoveries one makes. I had taken the water hyacinth to be just another plant one picks up at the nursery until someone's stray comment about what a miraculous plant it was led me to explore it a little further. A few hours of bouncing around the Internet made me realize that I was dealing casually with one of the planet's major desperadoes. It might be a remarkable purifier of water for my bog and pond, but many people call it the worst aquatic plant in the world.

Eichhornia crassipes is a plant of formidable fertility, being able to double its mass in a couple of weeks of good sun. In one study of its growth, two plants in four months produced over a thousand daughter plants, which in turn . . . It grows so fast that it can outrun all methods of control humans have so far devised. From its home in tropical South America it has now spread to more than fifty countries on five continents and is a major problem in tropical and subtropical waters around the world. The huge mats of living and decaying water hyacinth can build up to six feet thick. One acre can deposit about 500 tons of decaying material into its host waters in a year.

Water hyacinth was introduced into the United States at the 1884 Cotton States Exhibition in New Orleans and was much admired for its lovely violet to purple flowers, each with a bright yellow mark. At the conclusion of the exhibition, visitors were invited to take the remaining plants home. Bad move. Since then, it has spread unstoppably across the southern states. By 1895, floating mats more than twenty-five miles long had clogged St. John's River in Florida and blocked the steamboats.

In Africa it is becoming a major drain on some countries' resources, and large-scale World Bank projects are attempting to bring it under control. Lake Victoria is around 27,000 square miles, and in 1996 water hyacinth covered about 1 percent of it. Within three years it covered 3 percent. In Asia . . . well, you can use your search engine to explore further. But all this gave me more respect for the bulbous floating plants, and gratitude that these wanderers from the Amazon seem happy to sit in my Canadian gravel bog and clean the water for the fish. Our cooler climate also ensures that it doesn't reproduce itself so enthusiastically and doesn't survive our colder winters without help and indoor warmth.

The stream and waterfalls

The first artificial fountains and waterfalls were built for Persian emperors in what is now Iran about 4000 B.C. For much of the ancient world, west and east, natural springs have had a magical or numinous quality, as well they might. Water is where we started from: our oldest home. We left the sea only when we grew a bag of skin to carry our liquids within us. Often the springs of our ancestors were decorated with statues of gods or goddesses, and the names of many of the world's rivers derive from ancient divinities.

The more one looks at moving water, the more magical it seems. Think of Leonardo, watching and watching, and trying to draw the shapes in which it moved. If we see it little, or attend to it carelessly, then the magic is not so obvious. Flaubert put it better: "Everything is interesting, provided you look at it for long enough." I heard of an old woman who had lived all her life in a small village in the middle of England. A grandson with a new car discovered that she had never seen the sea. The next Sunday he arranged to take her to Blackpool, on the Lancashire coast. He walked with her out to the end of the pier, and the old woman stood in silence watching the sea for ten minutes or so, then turned to her grandson and said, "Is that all it does?"

I'm afraid I fell into the worst of my Irish habits building the stream. Instead of cutting a clean piece of liner from the remaining acres of the stuff, I decided to make do with various pieces left over from trimming around the pond, overlapping them so the water would flow merrily from one piece to another before becoming the final gurgling waterfall.

I started at the pond end, and dug the soil high behind the layers of stones already in place where the main waterfall into the pond was to be. Then I shaped a groove for the stream to go from the bog to the pond, and laid the irregular pieces of liner over it. Well, what a mess. But, it was show time. Everything seemed ready. I couldn't put it off any longer. There was nothing else to do but plug in the pump to the long and sturdy extension cord I had trailed from the house along the fence. My wife did the ceremonial job of connecting the power. We stood back, watching expectantly, and . . . nothing happened.

I don't know what I expected immediately. I thought I'd hear the pump, but there was nothing. No sound, no motion of water in the pond to suggest it was working. What to do

Susanna plugs in the pump.

now? I had not reckoned how long it would take to fill the bog. But finally it filled and overfilled, and the water came pouring murkily into the stream, and into the pond. The murk seems to have been due to a couple of bags of pea-gravel I

The stone-heavy stream. Moby Rock is in the right foreground, and the wall above is supporting the bog.

hadn't washed adequately. The water cleared in a few minutes, leaving me, though, with a rather soiled pond.

The next morning I got up to find the water level had dropped significantly. I poured in more from the hose. The next day it was down again. There must be a leak. It didn't take long to find that the water was seeping through every little gap in the liner along the stream, cunningly flowing back under the layers I had thought were carrying it onward. I had built a series of short stretches with slight backward slopes, so that, even if the pump stopped, there would be water to protect the liner from the sun. There were also three small waterfalls; one from the bog, another halfway along the stream, and then the final fall to the pond. The main leaking culprit was the area of flowback just below the bog.

So I did what I should have done at the beginning. I threw

aside the old pieces of liner and cut a generous chunk of clean liner from the acreage so far untouched. I spread the single new piece, tucking it far under the wide lip that came out from the bog and stretching down to the very edge of the falls into the pond. The next day, there was no discernible loss of water. Now I could start laying stones over the liner and begin elaborating the pretense that this combination of technologies was a part of the natural world.

four

Bringing life to the pond

The pump was working, some tall plants were on the marginal shelves, oxygenators were on the bottom and floaters on the surface; now I could look forward to adding fish, which would bring further life to the pond. I spent a day laying out the plants, adding gravel to the bog, netting leaves or bits of grass from the pond surface, and basically getting it ready to install the new tenants, perhaps even the next day. I went to bed tired but happily anticipating the golden flash of fish among the green.

The attack of the raccoons
The following morning I found instead that those incorrigible desperadoes of suburban gardens, the raccoons, had wrecked my handiwork. The water lily had been upended and tossed off its base into the bottom of the pond. The floating plants were in tatters, having been chewed and mostly discarded by those fastidious gourmands. They had toppled the tall marginal plants and sampled some for their potential gustatorial delights. A test the plants had clearly failed.

How could I put fish into the pond if raccoons were likely to have a nightly swim and frolic, and make a sushi meal of little goldfish? Once again, what to do? I asked neighbors, each of whom had a suggestion. One had heard that pepper kept them away. I bought a couple of large tins and spread it all around the pond. It did seem to deter the raccoons, but it deterred me too. A visit to the pond was followed by a sneezing bout. And I couldn't keep adding pepper—what would the place be like after five years?

Others recommended rigging up a small electric shock wire, which seemed a bit much in an area full of cats and visited by grandchildren. My elder son, ever practical, suggested land mines. "They'd learn after the first few." But as Canada had taken the lead in getting signatories to the international landmine treaty, I didn't feel this was the way to go either. As a stopgap, I bought a pile of eight-foot-long 1" × 2"s, and a roll of chicken wire. I made three large frames that would reach across the pond, stapled the chicken wire to them, and lowered them over the pond each evening.

In the fastness of the night, I have occasionally heard something—presumably frustrated raccoons looking for their sushi fix—jiggling the frames. They have held for a number of months now, but I'm not eager to have to cover the pond each night for the rest of my life, and uncover it on wet or snowy mornings. And the raccoons, I have learned, are not the only predators that see ponds as snack bars.

Finishing the pond with fish

After a few weeks of the oxygenating plants settling in and beginning to grow, and the water lily sending up tentative buds, and the floating water hyacinths spreading, and water lettuce trailing long wispy roots, and the pump pumping with Teutonic efficiency, and no signs of the raccoons getting past the chicken-wire frames—it seemed time for the fish.

My wife and I went into one of those pet supermarkets, thinking they might have the greatest variety, and viewed a wall of multicolored fish. There seemed to be a discouraging number of belly-up floaters. The shop seemed to hire only very young people, no doubt at minimum wage, whose real lives appeared to be going on elsewhere. When I pointed out some belly-up fish, the young woman who had been least reluctant to help me desultorily scooped them out with a net and carried them away for what I feared would be less than an honorable burial. I was looking for simple goldfish, like the ones we used to win at the fairground when we were children—for flipping ping-pong balls into the open necks of the small round bowls the fish swam in. It was almost impossible, of course, but now and then by some miraculous fluke, and much to the attendant's chagrin, a ball would bounce around and settle on the water of a bowl. A thousand years ago.

Peering into one tank after another, I couldn't find a simple goldfish. First I eliminated all the tropical fish for indoor aquariums, which was most of the wall. I was left with maybe ten or a dozen tanks of outdoor fish. But even those that looked more or less like goldfish were red and white or multicolored or exotically shaped. I didn't want koi, as the pond seemed too small to house the juicy monsters these might become in a few years. Here I was, no longer the little boy who, with freezing hands, carried a goldfish home from the fair in a bowl. I had the money to afford what I wanted but was unable to find the simple goldfish of yore. Obviously some parable there. I didn't mind that they wanted $10 or $15 each for these exotic beauties. I would have paid more for just regular goldfish.

Rather plaintively, I fear, I asked whether they didn't have anything more ordinary. After I had examined each tank with the apparently tranquilized young woman, and after I asked repeatedly for something more like a regular goldfish, she floated away smiling vaguely, to be replaced by a young Asian man. He edged toward me, perhaps as the result of some signal from the young woman, whereby they passed around hopeless customers. After going through the same routine of showing me the exotic fish and saying how great each was, and my again constantly asking for just a simple goldfish, he said, rather mysteriously, that there was another possibility.

Looking around a bit furtively, he sneaked me into a narrow room at the end of the wall of fishes, into which the young woman had earlier borne the corpses. Inside was an enormous tank crowded with gazillions of little goldfish, exactly what I was looking for. He was clearly disappointed at my delighted face, and told me these were "feeder fish," and I could have them for twelve cents each.

"Why are they called feeder fish?" I asked.

With a look of bewilderment at my naiveté, he said, "Because we sell them as food for bigger fish and turtles."

When I seemed surprised, I think he concluded he was dealing with a potentially unstable crazy. I realized that nature red in tooth and claw had to be accommodated even in pet supermarkets, but, even so, the commercialization of producing feeder fish for other more expensive fish seemed a tad grotesque.

I described the size of my pond and asked how many I should get, so they would feel comfortable and not too crowded or too few. I had been imagining ten or a dozen, but he recommended I take one hundred. So I did.

He slurped about a hundred into a large plastic bag, and my wife and I zoomed home to get them into the pond before they died for lack of oxygen or from poisoning themselves with their own excreta. The nitrogen kills them. That's why the pond has been crammed with oxygenating plants and a pump that delivers nitrogenous stuff to the bog where it will be extracted by the bog plants even as it fertilizes them, I hope.

We rested the bag on the pond for ten minutes or so, then opened it up and let a little pond water mix with the water in the bag. We were distressed to see that three or four of the fish were already dead. We waited for a while longer, gradually adding more pond water, and checking to see that the temperature in the pond was about the same as that in the bag, then we gradually released them, and the pond came to life. They took off, zoomed around, dove down to the bottom; some hung around the shelf where we released them, but on the whole they seemed happy to explore. We left them to it, covering the pond with the chicken-wire frames for the night.

The next day there was another dead fish. Two days later a couple more. For the next few weeks they were dying two or three a day sometimes. I scooped them out and gave them an inadequate burial. The only consolation was my wife's assurance that their few days or weeks of life in the pond were likely happier than the fate they were due for in the shop or serving their grisly role as feeder fish. But what was I to do? Was the pond contaminated in some way? Or were the fish diseased, and were they all going to die?

I prepared a hospital bucket—with oxygenating plants and sprinklings of food—into which I put any fish that showed symptoms of disease. (I should interject here that I have tended to anticipate a life somewhat more like James Bond's than any of this would suggest. But somehow the guns and gleaming women seem to be receding as goldfish and water hyacinth intrude themselves into my imagination.) Some of the fish had fluffy growths, some just got torpid and floated helplessly, giving a reluctant kick if approached too close. Nothing survived the sick bucket for more than a couple of days. Should I empty the rest of the fish out of the pond? But where to put them? In the midst of all this death and dismay every morning—my peaceful pond a scene of megadeath—I had to go to Hong Kong for about ten days.

My wife's e-mails while I was away assured me the deaths were fewer and fewer. After I came back, there seemed to be hardly any deaths. The remaining fish—only about thirty—

seemed to be thriving, growing, and energetic. I went to a small local fish shop—Noah's Pet Ark—and asked what I should do. I didn't want to add more fish until I was sure the pond was healthy. I was told that I could medicate it, at a stupendous cost, or I could feed the fish some medicated pellets, which I bought. I was also assured that there was normally a significant death rate for these feeder fish in late spring.

"You should see how they come," the large young woman in the shop said.

"From where?"

"China. In tanks with thousands of them crammed together." She sounded outraged.

She thought it would be safe to add new fish after there had been no deaths for a couple of weeks. Our younger son had come along to buy me a birthday present of four shibunkins. Sturdy-looking brutes, blue and black with spots of red, and long graceful tails. My sister-in-law also wanted to buy some fish for my birthday, so four white and red-blotched sarasas were added, and my other son contributed another four shibunkins. There hasn't been a death now for many weeks, and the menagerie drift and dart to and fro in the pond, nibbling the algae beginning to proliferate on the liner, exploring the pond generally, sometimes sitting under the waterfall where I suppose the water comes in oxygen-rich. I feed them a little each morning after removing the chicken-wire frames, so they now gather, mouths a-gobble, near wherever I stand, as though they hadn't eaten for a week.

But the anxieties of caring for a fish-full pond never cease. The other morning I came down to find the biggest and greediest shibunkin with a horrible-looking growth in its mouth, dull gray and half an inch long. When the fish came to the surface, trying to get at the food I had sprinkled, its mouth was working away at the growth—it looked like some kind of larva. I phoned Noah's Pet Ark again, but none of the

The stars of the pond and the water poppy.

young women I talked to had ever heard of anything like the
mouth growth I described. "Catch the fish, then pull whatever
it is out with tweezers," the most authoritative young woman
suggested. Easy for her to say. It took me an hour to catch the
fish, maneuvering two nets. I'm not sure how James Bond
would have dealt with this. It was not only the biggest fish
but also the smartest. I could have caught any number of the
others, as they gathered to admire the net, and nibble at it.
But the shibunkin was fast and elusive. I circled the pond, as
did the fish. But I finally got it. I kept it in the net and laid it
among the stones under the water at the shallow shelf. I then
tried to get at the thing in its mouth as it thrashed. Finally I
got the gray lump between the tweezers, and pulled gently.
Out came a whole four-inch worm, which had clearly gone
for a walk and drowned. The shibunkin had bitten off more

than it could chew, and then couldn't get it in or out. Once the dead worm was removed, the shibunkin swam happily away. ("How do you know he was happy?" "How do you know that I don't know . . . ?")

High winds and crashing plants

I read that one should fertilize the "marginal" plants sitting in pots on the shelf around the pond. The top of each pot was a few inches below the water level, with a couple of inches of gravel over the soil to prevent the soil seeping away and murking up the pond. The fertilizer came in the form of hard, round pellets, which one pushes in through the gravel and down to the roots, using thumb or finger, as long as one doesn't fear snapping thumb or finger while thrusting the sharp-edged pellets down through the resisting gravel and soil. While getting the fertilizer to the plants' roots proved painful, the grateful plants responded within a few days with impressive growth. I had bought a couple of pots of splendid variegated flags, with long graceful stems, and some bulrushes, sedge, umbrella plants, papyrus, and a few pots of miniature bamboo.

The plants grew taller and taller, and looked perfect at the rear of the pond. Early in the summer we had a day of high winds. The few early-fallen leaves were swirled around, and the cheerful gusts romped through the trees and plants. Looking for something else to play with, the wind pulled the tall marginal plants to and fro, and friskily toppled them into the water. I came home that day to find the pond muddied and tops of the plants trailed across the surface.

The added sludge had caught in the pump filter, reducing the waterfall to half its usual flow. Being a bit harassed and short of time, I thought I'd first try to clean the filter while the pump was working, instead of turning it off to do the job. Every week or so I'd been removing the filter and swishing it around in a bucket of water to clean it, so I could now do it

Marginal plants on a rainy day.

efficiently in a couple of minutes. I sat on one of the flat stones at the side of the pond and pulled on the hose, hauling the pump up to the shelf where the marginals had been, making sure to keep the pump under the surface. With one hand I slipped off the filter and began swishing it around in the bucket of water.

The fish had become very tame and associated a human figure sitting by the pond with feeding time. I was suddenly panicked to see them all gathering around the pump. Without the filter, the fish could be sucked into the pump! What could I do? I couldn't pull the pump out of the water as that would wreck the motor, and I couldn't leave the pump there pumping while I ran to the switch—thirty feet away—as I might lose a dozen fish to a grisly fate. The fish clearly thought this was a new form of feeding, or perhaps they were just feeling sociable, as it seemed all forty of them gathered round, heading lemming-like for the pump intake. Then I heard a horrible sucking sound and the pump groaning. Was that a fish? I put the pump down on the shelf, splashed the water to shoo the fish away, and scrambled to unplug the pump as fast as I could. I got back to see the water flowing out of the pump as the pressure from the bog reversed the flow. No fish parts evident! I cleaned the filter at more leisure, slotted it back on, and then, maneuvering the stiff hose, lowered the pump onto its watery throne of gray bricks and switched it on again. After a minute or so the bog filled and the water poured over the waterfalls, danced cheerfully among the stones, and threw itself musically into the pond.

I still find it hard to resist the irrational expectation that the constantly tumbling waterfall must soon overflow the pond, like a tap one forgets to turn off in the bathroom. It is such a simple system, pumping the water up to the bog and letting it run down again to the pond. But, of course, the planet works on a fairly similar system, sucking water off the oceans, dropping it on the land, and letting it find its way back down to the oceans. Many a philosopher in days of yore must have sat by major rivers watching the mighty, endless flow into the sea, wondering where it was all going.

The solution to the toppled plants was to repot them into wider and heavier plastic baskets. I'd kept them in the pots I had bought them in, and hadn't noticed that roots were pushing out the bottom, and in one case overflowing the top too.

I had anticipated that repotting would be a tedious chore, especially as I was now beginning to think about building the teahouse—hammering and sawing and bolting and cementing—but it proved to be surprisingly pleasant on a sunny Sunday afternoon in summer, sitting (sibilantly) in a garden chair, repotting water plants. I have never been the kind of person who dreamed that such an activity would ever figure among his pleasures. My daydreams used to be more in the "Oh the pearl seas are yonder" line of romantic adventure than in domestic ministration to green bog weeds. But there I sat through the slow afternoon, with buckets of water, heavy wet soil, and chunks of gravel, entirely happy with my very small realm of action.

The job involved slipping part of a garbage bag into a square, thin-mesh-sided plastic container for water plants. The garbage bag material would minimize soil seeping into the water, and I punched some holes in it to allow water to seep into the roots. With a trowel I dug from a large bag of specially formulated rich heavy soil that wouldn't be tempted to float out of the container and take a runner all around the pond. I then plopped a couple of fertilizer tablets into the soil and slipped the tall plants from their plastic pots and settled them into these much larger and heavier containers. I covered the soil with a couple of inches of attractive granite gravel and carefully lowered them one by one, as the shadows lengthened, onto the deepest part of the marginal shelf at the rear of the pond.

In the middle of gently encouraging gravel to settle among the stalks, I received a harried phone call from a colleague in Hong Kong. It was Monday for him, and while I sympathized with his problems, I can't deny that the call added a tiny dimension of pleasure to my idle afternoon's messing about with plants.

Disaster strikes!

The following weekend, I had too much to do at my desk. All of it seemed urgent, but I couldn't decide, among the many urgent items, which to start on, so I went out to uncover the pond. The water had not cleared since the high winds had toppled the tall plants and spilled much of the soil from their pots, producing murky green-brown mud and algae. I began moving a stone here and there, found a bit of moss and patched it into the moss garden, which I discuss in Chapter 5. There seemed to be a lot to do here as well. I had to get back to my desk, but first I began washing piles of the multicolored stones they call drain-rock in the wheelbarrow. Then I spread them in the small trench around the outside edge of the pond—so that overflow or heavy rains wouldn't carry muddy water into the pond, but let it drain through the stones into the soil. I then moved a few of the water plants from the surface of the pond and, pushing my fingers slowly down through the wet gravel of the bog, eased the roots in after them. The water hyacinths in particular would consume the nitrogenous materials taken from the pond by the pump, and they are also, as I discovered from the Internet, amazing consumers of noxious minerals. The bog looked better with the further set of green and bulbous water hyacinths growing on the damp gravel. One thing led to another—pruning a bit here, shifting some of the basalt stones around the moss garden to give a smoother slope down to pond level, cutting back some weak bamboo culms, and so on—till the day was nearly over.

My last job was to fill in patches of still water in the bog. I was concerned that they might provide a happy breeding ground for mosquitoes. They wouldn't breed in the pond, as the fish would get them, mosquito larvae being their favorite food. Nor where the water was moving in the stream and waterfall. But those still areas at the back of the bog looked like possible sources for mosquitoes. I had a half bag of gravel left over—an attractive mottled pile of subtly colored stones. I used it to fill in all the exposed bits of water, then piled it around the edges to hide any remaining bits of liner I could see, finishing by tossing the last handfuls around to cover any remaining watery spots. By the end of this desultorily industrious day, the undone tasks on my desk seemed much less urgent than they had in the morning.

The next day I came out early to relieve the pond of the protective chicken-wire frames, which seemed to be successful in keeping raccoons from the water. I had to rush off to a meeting I couldn't miss. But the pond was more than half-empty! The fish were in a murky foot or so of water, liner exposed all around, the water lily's leaves drooping down around its exposed pot. What to do? A sudden leak somewhere! Where? How?

Luckily, I had filled a garbage can of water and a pail the night before, to let the chlorine dissipate, so I poured them in. I calculated that if it had taken all night to get to this point, I could make it to my meeting and be back before too great a disaster occurred. But that was little comfort, as I had no idea where the leak was occurring. If it was the pond, I should get the fish out now and into the garbage bin, dumping a lot of the oxygenating plants in first. But perhaps it was in the bog—in which case I would have to dig out the tons of stones. And where would I put them while I looked for the leak? Or was it in the stream? That seemed less likely after my fixing the earlier leak. What to do? I pulled the plug that connected the pump to the power line, and the waterfall slowly ceased. I noted the level at which the water stood. If it was the same when I got home, then I'd know the leak was not from the pond itself, but in the bog—a conclusion I dreaded.

The meeting was slow to begin. Colleagues who hadn't seen each other for a while were chatting expansively, one handing around photographs of where he had been on holiday in Italy. I could think only of the fish, imagining the water continuing to dribble away while these people idly talked. When the meeting finally got under way, I was impressed that I was able to contribute to the discussion at all. As the talk went to and fro across the table, with handouts of charts I found hard to focus on, I had one of those flashes of vision. When I had poured gravel onto the patches of standing water at the edge of the bog, I had drawn the water in the bog to a new level! Before it could flow to the outlet at the lip of the bog, it was finding the top edge of the liner at the rear of the bog! I hoped.

The meeting over, a couple of colleagues wanted to dissect what had gone on and enjoy some gossip about the behavior of one of the nuttier contributors to the discussion. After smilingly extricating myself, I still faced some paperwork I had to get done, then a computer problem that I had to deal with. Doubly frustrating problems, as I was aching to get home.

I sped, constrainedly, across town, rehearsing my options. I couldn't escape the image of flailing fish in inches of sludge. Up the drive at incautious speed, braking hard before taking out the fence, then a rapid gallop out to the pond. The water level was no lower. I went round to the rear of the bog. The water had been turned off so it wasn't spilling over the liner now, but I could see that the soil where I had imagined the problem was indeed saturated, and even the path in the rear showed signs of heavy damp. I turned the pump on again, waited for the water to rise up in the bog, and lo and behold, there it was dribbling out at two points. I pulled away the gravel, and the water level in those areas lowered. I scraped out pretty much all the gravel I had put in the previous day.

But what to do now? I couldn't simply pour water into the pond, as the chlorine content would be toxic to the fish. Also, it had been a warm day, and the remaining water in the pond was quite warm, and the cold water from the hose would put them into shock. I had bought a small bottle of dechlorinating liquid, so I filled one garbage can full and mixed in a few dechlorinating drops—hoping it wasn't too much. The bottle carried the cheerful warning that too much could be as toxic as too little. It indicated that 50 cc would deal with 1,000 gallons. How many drops for a garbage can? Or a pail? I suspect in my hurry I overdid it. I poured in the pailful and emptied the garbage can a pailful at a time. The fish seemed to be delighted, as the stream of water dislodged the brown, caked algae from the side of the pond. Dinner was served.

I began to fill the garbage can again, and, while the tap water poured in, I rushed in and out of the house and up and down the garden with pails of hot water, to try to minimize the shock of temperature differences. As with children, one didn't look for thanks. I was reminded out of the blue that my mother had once said in this garden, when she was visiting, that children owed their parents nothing. I think this is indeed how parents, but not children, should think about it. My fish owed me no gratitude either. This is what can make keeping fish good for us.

After an hour of this frenzied activity, and getting the pond a little fuller, I had the inspiration of phoning the Noah's Pet Ark, from where I had bought the recent set of shibunkins. I could, no doubt, have phoned the pet supermarket, but had little confidence the kids who were dealing with calls there would have any idea. But at the local specialist shop—which I swear I will patronize exclusively in future—Anna answered and sympathized with my dilemma, and the edge of panic still in my voice. First, I needn't worry too much about the chlorine. I could take the garden hose, and spray it high into the air to fall back into the pond. Nearly all the chlorine would be dissipated by the contact with the air. It was a warm day, and the fish would be able to handle the small drop in temperature the new water would add. But she casually mentioned another variable that encouraged panic again, telling me I needed to add baking soda to the water to neutralize the acid. Our local water, it seems, is more acidic than fish can easily survive, and replacing more than half the water should be balanced by an alkaline agent. How much? A teaspoon per 100 gallons. And how does that work out per garbage can? Yikes. I put in a few spoonfuls, stirred it, and spread it around the pond, to make up for the hundreds of gallons I had put in so far.

By the time my wife came home, the water was halfway back to where it had been, but, even so, she was shocked. She immediately started toting pails of hot water to minimize the stress on the fish—regardless of the stress on us. By the early evening, my panic was all dissipated like the chlorine, and I sat in a chair in the shade of the apple trees aiming a spraying jet of water into the blue sky, which fell as a gentle rain from heaven onto the pond. The fish were delighted. ("How do you know . . . ?" "How do you know that I don't know . . . ?")

The next morning all seemed well. The fish were still all alive and the water was only five or six inches below normal. As I mentioned, I occasionally compare my life with James Bond's, and it can be a sobering few moments. But the tensions of the seeping water, the need to make decisions on the run, with inadequate information and lives at stake, adrenaline pumping and heart going hard—when I had the leisure to notice it—all seemed to me fairly reminiscent of the Bond style. I concede a few differences, which needn't be spelled out, and my technologies of pump and hosepipe, plastic garbage can and pail, don't quite stack up with what Q provides, but it was a Bond-like day in which boredom was far away. What is the meaning of life? Life has many meanings, and among them are the fish in our care.

Once the pond was back to full depth, and the fish seemed happy, the temptation of sitting by the pond returned—too often. I would go out and find my work time being increasingly preempted by the pleasure of sitting looking at the moss garden or watching the fish. It seemed I would never get the teahouse project under way.

But, as with most tasks, the trick was to begin. I needed a shovel and the wheelbarrow to get rid of the mound of clay first—my wife gave permission to pile it to the rear of the shrubs along the north-side fence. (A couple of years ago our neighbors on that side sold their house. Within days it was crunched and carted away in huge trucks, as is the practice here and now. In its place a palace was constructed, a pinkish confection rather out of tune with the rest of the houses, but no doubt our turn would come and something more in tune with the confection would go up in place of our house.) In the process of putting in a fence all around the new house, the new owners discovered that our neighbors had for decades appropriated, no doubt unknowingly, between two and three feet of our garden; an encroachment corrected by the new construction. So there was a chunk of empty ground behind the line of our shrubs. That space was to become the repository of the clay from the pond. The clay had by now been moved around a few times—from the base of the pond to the garden area on the right, then over to the left when I started building the waterfall. Once the design for that side was worked out, the clay was wheelbarrowed over to the empty teahouse site; now it was going to what I hoped would be its final resting place behind the shrubbery.

A granite border
Meanwhile, the shelf at the front of the pond was an unsolved problem. It was wide and flat, beautifully done—the best of those around the pond—but useless because it was too shallow. I hadn't realized when building it that one couldn't find plants that needed only four or five inches of water. And I hadn't realized, as I plastered the wet sand around the dugout pond, that I was raising the level of this shelf too much.

Sitting by the pond one day, I had another of those odd and sudden senses of what would solve the problem. I could have a mostly submerged stone garden on the shelf, perhaps with some small plants between the stones, and space for the fish to get around to eat up any mosquito larvae. I suppose, in a minor sense, it was an insight. That is, it wasn't a matter of working it out, or thinking it through, or coming to a conclusion. One finds suddenly that such ideas are already in one's mind, as though they have been slipped in fully formed while one was looking elsewhere.

I scoured around the garden again hunting for granite. For some reason, I had the notion that it was to be a granite border, but I decided to fill it out with other small stones. I began with the expensive stones that were to serve as ground-cover by the bamboo and under the teahouse. But under six inches of water among the granite, they looked dull. I tried the purple ones, but they too seemed washed out by the strong, bright granite. I finished up laying the drain-rock they sell in bags for next to nothing—the water brings out their varied colors, and they give the granite a good setting while not suppressing its glory.

Washing the stones was an aesthetic treat. The varied beauty of these colored stones was astonishing. How could anything so beautiful be available for so little in such quantity? Dribbling the stones onto the submerged shelf, I was further bemused by their smoothness, which one takes for granted. Those perfect rounded shapes were achieved over decades, or centuries, rolling down rivers, all their edges clacked away as the waters carried them on, gathered by currents into vast piles, dredged out and packed in plastic bags, and finishing ingloriously as drainage around houses, or, a little more gloriously, decorating middle-class Japanese-style gardens.

Sitting around the pond

Friends and relations now come out before dinner and sit around the pond to chat. People are kind in their appreciation, and often say how I must enjoy sitting here watching the goldfish among the floating plants, with the sound of the water running among the stones of the stream and falling into the pond. Well, yes and no, I want to say.

Oddly, the pleasure mainly comes through others' pleasure.

To have made something that seems to delight friends and relations is a delight. But when I sit here by myself, I see mainly what needs still to be done, or what needs correcting. Indeed, I can rarely simply sit without jumping up to move some stones, or scoop some leaves off the pond, or clip back a bit of the bamboo. If I do manage to sit still, I fret about whether the water quality is all right for the fish, or whether there is still a small leak behind the waterfall, or I fear that if the water gets too high it will bring soil into the pond and darken it, or that those stones really should be refitted. Other people look at the bog and seem to get pleasure from its wall and the wet gravel with the miniature bamboo and water hyacinth growing in it, but I see the layers of hidden stones, and worry whether any shift might crush the pipe at its base . . . and so on. You get the idea. Maybe as time goes by and it all continues to work, I will relax and see the surface that is delightful instead of the more rugged and makeshift substructures that hold this artifice together.

Some, being polite, say something like, "You did it all by yourself? All those stones, the wall, the plants?" I think these must be people who have never moved small things systematically until they become big things. This moving of a stone upon a stone can easily accumulate to a wall. People who have never worked systematically at a single project bit by bit, stone by stone, plank by plank, word by word, get an exaggerated awe before the pyramids. Just a stone upon a stone upon a stone. It's the persistence largely that differentiates the small half-done task from the wonder of the world. I do recognize some differences between the pyramids and this small garden. But when I respond to people who admire the garden excessively by saying it really isn't much work, just an irregular persistence toward a not complex project, they assume I am pretending modesty. But I'm not. We can all make greater works by just gradually accumulating the stone upon a stone, or the plank upon a plank, or another lousy word upon a word.

But what does give unalloyed pleasure is to see insects and birds, and the fish, taking this construction as a part of the natural world. I get much pleasure, even joy, from the squirrel that runs along the roof of the fence, the dragonfly resting on a water lily leaf, birds having an energetic bath in a shallow pool they have found or made in the bog, or the fish taking this artificial pond with its not well folded lining and German pump sitting on bricks, and the water lily on an upturned planter, as a fine natural home that provides adequate accommodation, food, light, and companionship . . . Well, you get that idea too. There are creatures who are finding it either an adequate home or a good place to visit. Including raccoons.

The first winter
The coming of spring was inexorable and decidedly pushy, ignoring entirely my work schedule and a trip that I had to make. And now at the other end of the summer winter comes flailing down October, scattering leaves in all directions, with no regard for the fact that I have to go to Ireland for a week and don't have time to get everything done. I am trying to build the teahouse and have slabs of plywood flooring probably killing the lawn on top of which they lie, warping in the damp, and the frost at the end of the month is already dusting the exposed area of the lawn. And now that November has begun, winter seems to think it needs no further excuse to begin wreaking havoc. I can't get on with the teahouse because I need to get the plants around the pond sorted out, as well as fight off the mountains of leaves that all seem to have a homing instinct for the pond and the more inaccessible crannies of the wall around the moss garden (described in Chapter 5).

I talked with a helpful young woman in an aquatic-plant place out in the country. I had seen it by chance. I was the only customer, as theirs is mainly a spring business. I wanted to buy some extra oxygenating plants for the winter. With a very kind voice, calm eyes, and a charming, gentle smile, she loaded me with a tight stomachful of extra anxieties. As she slowly and considerately lowered each hornwort plant into a plastic bag, I casually asked a few questions about some of the familiar plants in the huge greenhouse. I came away with a month-long list of things that were all urgent. Cut all the leafage off the water lily; it's hardy, so leave it in the pond. Dump all the floating plants in the compost; with a bit more frost they'll turn to mush and sink. Clean leaves from the bottom of the pond. Sink some pots or tubes so the fish can hide. Put a net over the top of the pond. Repot the umbrella plants and the gorgeous papyrus in a regular light soil, and bring them indoors, giving them plenty of light.

Now I set about these tasks in the time I had after work and before the sun set—an increasingly narrow time, and too often nonexistent. I had mental lists, to get pipe to sink in the pond, to pull out the marginal plants and repot them, to cut back the hardy ones that I could leave on the pond shelves, to buy a net for the pond, and so on. I first realized I was running around out of control and not thinking sensibly when I rushed at a series of jobs one late afternoon. I'd already bought some heavy plastic pipe to give the fish somewhere to hide from birds. It was six feet long, and I cut it into irregularly sized sections, which I lined up on the wall. I then began to stretch out the netting I had bought, imagining I would nail it to the base of the first row of posts that were to support the teahouse, stretch it across the pond, and fasten it around heavy stones at the other side. I had left the chicken-wire frames up during the day, so I began to move them to fit the netting in place and also to roll some of the pipe into the bottom of the pool.

It was about this point, as I lifted the first frame up, that I began to think. My first thought was something like, what on earth was I doing preparing three mutually redundant solutions to the problem of how to protect the fish? The netting did nothing more than the frames I had already built did—lying over the pond, collecting leaves, and keeping off predators. Indeed, the chicken-wire frames were probably more effective and sturdy than the netting would be. And if I had the frame, or the netting, over the pond, why did I imagine the fish would need pipes to dive into for protection? I put the frame back, packed up the netting, and have no idea what I can do with assorted chunks of black ABS pipe.

I was still sometimes uncovering the pond during the day. I'm not sure why, but I felt the fish might feel less claustrophobic—though I don't recall any fish psychoanalysts suggesting this was a common neurosis among goldfish. Sitting at my desk looking out over the pond one morning, my eye was attracted by some movement, and I looked up to see splashing and something taking off from the water. With the plants dying back, the fish were less protected. I went out and covered the pond, deciding to leave it so for the rest of the winter.

The following day I looked up to find a blue heron, three feet tall, sitting patiently by the side of the pond with its long fish-devouring beak ready for action. It seemed bewildered by the chicken-wire frames that were separating it from the fish. Undoubtedly, this had been my visitor of the previous day when the frames were not in place. As I went out and tried to take its picture, it took off.

So this chapter might also be called "Taking Life from the Pond." The next day I took a careful look at the fish, and indeed a number were missing, including "Worm," the big shibunkin. That my greedy, energetic friend had come to such an end in a heron made me feel like a negligent pond owner: I had left my poor fish defenseless.

five

The raised garden

ENGLISH GARDENS ARE DE-
signed for summer's space, for the warm days and long
evenings. Not a huge amount of thought is given to how the
garden will look in the winter. In the sodden English climate,
the garden is typically cut back in the late autumn and aban-
doned till spring begins to move the roots and seeds again.
Planning a Japanese garden requires giving thought to each
season equally. This doesn't mean that the garden has to look
the same in each season, but that it must offer to its partici-
pants throughout the year the qualities of mind and soul for
which it was designed.

A product of this all-seasonal approach is that you cannot
give too much space to plants that will flower profusely for just
a few months and then be uninviting to the eye. The only
items in the garden that do not significantly change with the
season are the stones. A Japanese garden may be designed
without a pond, without trees, without a teahouse, without
plants even, but it is inconceivable without stones.

The great gardens of the early period in Japan yielded to the
smaller scale domestic garden after the mid-thirteenth century,
with the expansion of a middle class. The austere, simplified,

and more abstract gardens, such as some of the more famous Kyoto temple gardens, were the result of Zen Buddhist influences during the fifteenth and sixteenth centuries. The refinements of Zen gardens led to the quest for greater simplicity, recognizing the beauty of the informal and irregular, and even the imperfect scattering of formal patterns that nature will always manage. So that search for aggressive neatness, order, and symmetry one finds in many Western gardens is deliberately undermined in the Zen garden. Some famous tea masters would say that the sweeping and cleaning of the garden should be given to a boy or an old man, because neither would be excessively scrupulous and neat.

My first experience of a Japanese-style garden was when visiting friends of my wife's mother; one of those occasions felt to be dutiful on both sides. They were wealthy, and the husband was a keen gardener, and had had an extensive garden landscaped. As my wife and I were shown around, we tried to keep to the orthodox irregular stones placed in gravel. But as there were four of us and we could hardly walk in line, this proved difficult. The result was that we occasionally scuffed pieces of gravel onto the stones. The husband walked behind with a brush, taking no part in the conversation, but carefully sweeping each piece of gravel off the stones in our wake. No wonder it took me a quarter century to be able to contemplate Japanese gardens as possibly enjoyable places.

I suppose I should have written something about *wabi-sabi* before this point, though I am unsure what to write. It is a central and commonly mentioned Japanese aesthetic principle, derived significantly from Zen Buddhist sources, but it lacks an easy definition. *Wabi* has been translated as simple quietude, and *sabi* as elegant simplicity. Together, they represent a reaction against those aesthetic principles, and styles of life and soul, that glorify symmetry, order, completeness, and so on. Wabi-sabi resists the appeal of clean, finished surfaces, of precise angles, and also of elaborate ornateness. It involves, by contrast, a recognition of the desirability of incompleteness, or irregularity, of unfinished and rustic surfaces, of the unpretentious and natural. In a room governed by wabi-sabi, there would be nothing outstanding, shown with pride at the expense of other things; all have a place, all are to be undemonstrative, and we are to delight in the imperfect, the incomplete, and the modest.

So I should not be struggling for smooth finishes, symmetry, and precise order—even if I could achieve any of them. The abuse of wabi-sabi is to see it as a negative principle—as failure to achieve a professional modern finish—instead of seeing it as beauty available to a refined sensibility that goes far beyond conventional good taste. The acceptance and delight in imperfection can seem confusingly close to the acceptance of the results of carelessness in one's work. But wabi-sabi and carelessness are really worlds apart, in more senses than one. Wabi-sabi is a positive austerity, whose principles I think will not really dominate my work. I suspect I would have to have greater skill to be able to construct according to wabi-sabi principles.

Beginning the garden

A small problem with the mechanics of this book is the difficulty of writing chronologically, moving from project to project as I did them. But it seemed better to describe one part of the project at a time, even though that means jumping around in time occasionally. At the beginning of this chapter and the following one, I go back in time prior to the completion of the pond. This chapter focuses on the building of the raised garden.

I had earlier built part of the retaining wall for the raised garden, just to have something against which to throw the soil I was digging out to make the strip in front of the fence where the black bamboo is now growing. By the time I began to work on the garden seriously, it was fall. Even unchanging stones suffer from decaying leaves settling over them. Overhanging the garden site is half of the birch tree from the condominium garden, and it began to drop early retirees onto the mounds of soil in September, with a wilting promise of tons more to follow. In high winds I watched them, like fallen angels diving down and turning my potential paradise into something that looked rather more like the other place. I was reminded of Milton's magical glimpse in *Paradise Lost* of the fallen angels "Thick as autumnal leaves that strow the brooks / In Vallombrosa." Except, it turns out, that Milton never visited Vallombrosa, a mountainside valley near Florence. If he had, he'd have seen that it was mainly wooded by conifers.

I was negotiating, as I've said, with the chair of the tenants' committee in the condominium to get the tree fork cut off— something I assumed I'd have to pay for. In the meantime I could go ahead with building up the wall and garden despite the leaves. For a while they would serve as compost, but I'd need to have them out of the way by the time the garden was complete. Tall birches are beautiful drifting trees from a distance, but they dribble sticky sap in the spring, drop strips of end-branches all summer, distribute a ton of seed, and then lose tons of leaves in the fall. No pond could survive the onslaught.

Negotiations with the tenants' committee of the condominium concluded with an agreement that they would take the tree out and that we would share the cost equally. So down it came one sunny autumn day.

Now I am the kind of person who reads, perhaps too much. And while I can't complain—I admit I have gained something from literature and can manage road signs—there are penalties for excessive literacy. So, taking on a good outdoor task like building a Japanese garden has meant that I have balanced the labor with reading books about Japanese gardens. And there are a lot (and now one more for anyone who might follow with the same affliction).

There is quite a variety of such books. I most like the ones that outline basic Japanese principles but seem willing to acknowledge that it is, in the end, your garden and you can do what you want. The other extreme includes books, usually by enthusiastic Americans who have made themselves experts, that severely rebuke the reader for any temptation to trespass outside the iron rules of Japanese gardening. They write with pursed lips and complex diagrams, laying down commands that you must follow or expect censorious groups of Japanese authorities, armed, to come knocking at your door in the night to exact revenge for your infringement of rules about the proper placing of stones.

I am a bit sensitive about these censorious books, not just because I can't always follow exactly how sets of scalene triangles determine how three stones ideally balance each other, but because I have broken a few rules. While I was still working on the fence, I kept my eyes open for appropriate plants for the garden area. I wanted things that would look good in all seasons, plants that would provide pleasant contrasts of shape and size, and one or two items that would be striking, in a Japanese kind of way. I had seen pictures of those pom-pom junipers, but whenever I found one in a nursery, it was bedraggled or mangy. Driving by a small nursery in the fall, I saw out of the corner of my eye a luxuriantly heavy-headed rich green pom-pom shrub by the side of the road. I pulled left into the next street, left, and left again, till I was back at the nursery. The juniper was just what I had been looking for.

The owner of the nursery came out. He was Asian, which somehow added authenticity.

"How much?" I asked.

"Two hundred dollars."

"Oh dear. Too much," I said regretfully.

"How much too much?"

Panic and calculation: What was the ideally right answer—which would save me most and not have him refuse to sell?

"One hundred dollars."

"Okay."

Damn. I should have tried for more. I drove home with the juniper barely contained in the trunk of the car, the big bobbed heads waving cheerfully at pedestrians. It was bigger than it had seemed by the roadside.

Later I was reading one of the more reproachful books. A chapter on "training" shrubs was largely taken up with instructions on torturing trees by constraining their roots, nipping their buds, or tying pieces of thick bamboo to their branches and hanging weights on them till they conceded and were crunched into the desired shape. After this, the author had the nerve to say that one should never have in one's garden one of those poodle-cut trees.

The uptight author claimed that you are allowed to accentuate or exaggerate the tree's or shrub's natural form but, he asserted, a tree that is poodled into heavy, dense tufts would hardly resemble the natural form of any species. Another book, to rub it in, talked about those "insensitively poodled" trees. Heigh-ho. Well, one can see their point, of course—the dwarfing of bonsai and the bud nipping and weighting *could* just about happen in odd circumstances in nature, whereas no natural event could lead to stripping off the lower branches and rounding the greenery on the ends. One may interfere with a tree or shrub to exaggerate some natural form, but not to create an unnatural shape. But I had concluded some time ago that Nature is greatly overestimated as an ally in gardening. I say that, while also acknowledging that when we garden we become partakers in the deepest mysteries we face: of the turn of the year, of the growth and death of living things, of our strange place in nature.

But spring was coming when I made my first efforts in the garden and seemed unconcerned to delay because of my bad back—from all that digging. It was unconcerned that I hadn't yet got the pond sorted out. It was unconcerned that the garden area was not ready for planting. We have no choice but to cooperate with the terrible inexorability of time and the seasons that we can't outrun. One might be called to Zen contemplation of the cycles of life and how we are a part of them, but one can also fret at what still needs to be done, recalling again Dorothy Parker's "back comes Spring . . . and the ground all mucked up with plants." Well, in the present case, threatening to get mucked up with all the wrong plants.

Having dug the soil from the pond and built the wall to contain it, I now had to decide what to do with this raised garden. There are two general kinds of Japanese garden. In the Tsukiyama style, small hills and stones and shrubs represent mountains and their forests and trees, and a pond represents the ocean. And in the Karesunsui style, sand represents the ocean, lines of stones represent rivers, and standing stones are mountains. This latter is the style that became prominent with the influence of Zen Buddhism and its monastery gardens. Given the rainforest setting of my garden, I felt less inclined to try to replicate, however inadequately, the sparse elegance and strange harmony of the monastery garden of Ryoan-ji. I'll visit Kyoto to enjoy that. I was more inclined toward stony verdure, lush evergreens amid stones, rounded box or privet and short spiky plants.

Except for these vague ideas, the garden was unplanned. Before long, the bog invaded the area, and the stream cut the garden into two parts. That gave me a small high patch beside the bog, where I decided to plant the pom-pom tree, a longer but narrow curved patch from the bog down to the edge of the pond, largely hidden by the white mass of Moby Rock and slabs of liner, and an irregular slice between the bog wall and the pond, which had the hose snaking across it.

Between the pond and the bog wall. The problem is what to do with this small stretch that will give it a Japanese flavor.

The moss garden

By chance, visiting Japanese gardening Web sites, I saw a reference to moss gardens and discovered that an amazing number of sites are dedicated solely to these tiny undemanding plants. And there, suddenly, was the idea that I should make one of the two remaining chunks of garden space a moss garden. I began by setting some of the larger stones — gathered from earlier digging — along the curving strip to the right of the stream. This did some damage to the knees, but created the basic shapes around which I could lay moss.

I had some time earlier bought the one concession to color in the garden, so far. This was a miniature rhododendron ('Baden Baden'). I planted it near the top of the curve toward the bog, and also added a few Korean rock ferns. They are small and will remain so. I also put in a couple of exotic heathers (*Erica arborea*) called 'Estrella Gold', which, the label says, will grow to four feet tall. Around these, and the stones, I would pack a carpet of soft green moss.

'Estrella Gold' in the moss garden, with 'Baden Baden' farther up, crouched apparently happily in the same long bed of moss. An edge of Moby Rock is visible at the bottom left, and the large stone beyond the Estrella heathers is one I moved, with some damage to the knees, from the front of the house.

I began hunting down chunks of moss around the garden. I discovered three kinds and decided on the most plentiful variety, which had made a home under shrubs and in the shade of fences, under ferns and behind the house—anywhere the sun didn't get. Having spent years cursing the prolific moss and trying to kill the damn stuff, raking it out of the lawn each spring, I now found myself treasuring every couple of square inches I could find. I was particularly irritated when I found a patch that had been invaded by spikes of that damn lawn grass growing through it. How to pull the grass out, without breaking apart the beds of moss, was the challenge now.

I was having to be furtive, sneaking under my wife's plants when she was out, slicing under thick pads of moss, and liberating them to what was an inch-by-inch and foot-by-foot accumulating moss garden. My fear was that my eagerness to get at the moss might be undermining some of her plants. I was careful to add shovelfuls of soil wherever I seemed in danger of exposing roots.

My harvesting of the rapidly depleted stock of these valuable small green plants became more desperate. I rapaciously loaded every square inch I could find onto my shovel and planted it around the stones, but I was running out of moss and was far from covering the space available. I had to become more furtive. The neighbors' garden to the south had lush chunks up against our fence, and under shrubs in their border. It seemed fair game to lean over the fence and pull up a shovelful, as these beds of moss were continuous with those on our side of the fence. But even when I had cleaned out all I could reach, there was still a discouraging acreage of soil showing in the lower half of what was beginning to look like a moss garden. Further toward the edge of their border, under shrubs and plants, I could see rich patches of lush dark green.

I knew how those Klondike guys felt about the shine of gold in rocks. Moss had come to seem like the most precious thing in the garden. Knowing that the neighbors, who had just bought the house and weren't yet moved in, were not there, my lust for more moss drove me to skulk into their garden, guilty spade at the ready. They wouldn't want moss growing in their border anyway, I assured myself. I was doing them a favor. And they'd never know it had been there. So the moss garden crept a further couple of feet toward the pond, flowing around the large stones and beginning to converge on Moby Rock.

But I had run out of moss, and there were feet to go. I wandered around, scooping out tiny pieces I had missed earlier. The front garden! I had forgotten the front of the house, and the dark patches under ferns and trees. It was like suddenly viewing a treasure galleon adrift on the ocean near one's island home. But these large patches were along the edge of the lawn and mostly had clumps of grass growing through them, which needed eradicating.

Between bouts of moss hunting, I would sit of an evening with my laptop computer on my knees, surfing Internet sites dedicated to moss. I learned that there are around 9,200 varieties, which makes the three I could locate in our garden a pretty paltry showing. I couldn't find examples of the kind I have used, so I don't know its name. It isn't Irish or Scotch, which are the two I recognize, but one of the 9,198 others.

The two-needle black pine
You may have been able to tell, from my aggressive reaction to the books that sniffily told me that my pom-pommed, poodled juniper was in poor taste and offensive to Japanese gardening principles, that I was vulnerable to the criticism. And the criticism rankled, mainly because I could see it had merit—otherwise why get irked? Well, there I was as the months progressed, irked and rankled, and increasingly dissatisfied with the inoffensive juniper. A significant problem with it—and I don't

even now want to confess that the purists' criticisms influenced me—was that the pom-poms all hung over around the same level, and as I had placed it at the top of the garden by the bog, it didn't show its individual bobbles to best effect. They tended to blur into one another. In fact, the plant showed best when one looked down on it rather than up to it. What I needed up there was something dramatic that gave height to that side of the raised garden.

I looked in the yellow pages for places that sold evergreen and ornamental trees. One place, outside the town in a suburb I had yet to enter without getting lost, said they had a number of two-needle Japanese black pines. I drove over, and indeed they had acres of shrubs and trees. And there stood a set of half a dozen magnificent pines of just the kind I was looking for. They were each about five to six feet tall. But would they fit the space I had by the bog? And how much were they? $450?! Plus $40 for delivery.

I couldn't afford that. But then it turned out, thanks to you, that I could. It was about this time that this book was accepted, and the publisher generously sent me a check as an advance on future royalties. So, I decided that, dammit, I was going to get one of these splendid bonsai-ed pine trees after all. The really sneaky part was that because I was now working at something that had a reasonable prospect of making money, I could write off all the costs against tax, and so the pine seemed almost a bargain.

Outside the shed that served as the office stood a wizened, weathered old Japanese man. As I asked him about the trees, he looked at me through crinkled smiling dark eyes. If you wanted a picture of the perfect ancient sage, here he stood, eyes looking at mine with a luminous intelligence. He nodded slowly as I spoke, encouraging me to go on further about what I was looking for and where it was to fit. I stopped and waited for his reply, and we looked at each other for a moment in silence. He paused, then seemed ready to tell me what was surely going to be some insight into the nature of pine-things or human life in general, but then gestured at his son approaching on a tractor. The old man didn't speak English. The son spoke it with confidence. We circled the set of pines. They were twenty years old, had been bonsai-ed and would grow very little more for the next twenty years. They had appealing arms and tufts of green needles like deep plates on the end of each branch. I felt I was going from pom-pom poodling to plates, at considerable cost, but the trees were evocative of Japanese styles I had seen in many pictures. The problem was whether the bole of roots would fit into the space I had. We agreed that I should go home, measure the space, and then come back and choose my tree.

The pom-pom juniper would look fine, I thought, to the side and rear of the future teahouse, but I didn't want to put it there yet as it would likely get damaged by the careless-nesses I had come to recognize as ingredients of my style of building. I dug a hole for it in the middle of the vegetable garden, now cleared for the coming winter. My fear was that removing the juniper would destroy the bog. The bog was held in by stone walls on two sides, by the weight of soil and stones on the side where it flowed into the stream, and by the packed soil at the rear where the juniper sat. If I were to simply dig out the juniper, I could be removing the bog's support, and the weight of stones and water would tear through the liner and pour into the hole.

So, first, I drove about ten long bamboo poles I had bought for some since-forgotten reason down between the bog and the juniper. Then I added a couple of long metal rods and hammered some pieces of wood across them. I thought that this should be enough support, and then gingerly I dug out the juniper. It came up quite easily, its root bole still largely in the shape of the tub I had bought it in. I dragged it into a wheelbarrow and replanted it in the hole in the vegetable garden. I also dug up the maple I had been sold as an evergreen (evergreen till its leaves fell in October). I dug this in beside the juniper to await the completion of the teahouse. I spaded out as much soil as I dared from the hole by the bog, in preparation for the pine. I had a space of about two feet by a bit less than two feet. It would be tight.

A few days later I went back to the nursery and chose the tree I wanted. Neither of the men I had met previously was there, but this time I was helped by a big, tough-looking man who seemed like a samurai warrior out of place and time. He thought the tree would fit into the space I described, and at $450 one might expect him not to be too doubtful or irresolute. It would be $50 to deliver. I said it had been $40 last Sunday, so he shrugged and said $40. It would take two of them to deliver it, and they would show up later in the day.

He arrived with another man whom I had not seen on either of my two previous trips. The samurai looked at the hole, and told me to dig out more soil, pointing particularly at the bog side. I said I feared the bog collapsing. This he clearly felt was a weakling's fear, and he gestured that I should get to work while he wheeled the tree up the garden. The two struggled with it. Even allowing for the fact that the second man was anorexically slight, the samurai was also having trouble with the tree. It didn't seem to have that much more bulk than the juniper, but its root bole was much bigger, and it was maybe three feet taller.

"Which way round? Once in, it stay so. Decide now," the samurai commanded. He and his miniature helper held it on the wall by the hole. Alas, I thought I wanted it exactly the opposite way around from the way they held it. With much grunting, they slowly moved it round. Then I was told to dig out even more soil. I did so, and then the samurai took a spade and sliced away further at the thin support of the bog.

The hole ready for the pine. The two small bushes are privets, whose job is to grow up and hide the pipe carrying water from the pond to the bog. They will be helped by a more artful layout of the stones around the lip of the bog. The chaotic bundle of stones and messy moss in the foreground is a result of my beginning to make a moss garden on this east side of the garden, later moved over to the narrower section to the west of the stream.

The remaining problem was the bamboo canes I had supporting the bog. The two branches of the tree on the bog side had to be able to stretch out beyond the bamboo, so I pulled the bamboo sideways to enlarge the space where the branches could slide in. The other main obstacle to the root bole was the wooden supports I had slammed in place against the bamboo.

He said something in Japanese, and the sword carrier grabbed and pulled the first support, but the bamboo held, and I was instructed to pull the other. One doesn't quibble with one of nature's samurai, even though I was much less confident than he was that disaster wouldn't follow. I pulled it out, and all seemed to hold. He still wasn't convinced he had enough room, so he hacked some more soil away. Then the two of them with what was probably exquisite Japanese cursing eased the tree off the stones and tried to maneuver it into the space. It didn't go easily, and there was some tugging as a branch got caught in the fence and another in the quince, and when parts of the root bole stuck against the bamboo strips, and when branches had to be slotted between the bamboo poles. In each of these maneuvers, the aspect of the tree I had wanted to face the teahouse was turned a bit and then a bit more, until it finished up about 45 degrees from where I had wanted it. But with all the cursing and sweating and struggling, I didn't have the heart to point out this minor geographic problem, deciding that the tree looked good from all angles, and, as I'd had only a minute to decide, maybe fate would make as good an aesthetic choice as I had.

And then it was in. The samurai stood on the wall and kicked the top of the root bole down. But it was hindered on the bog side, so he wanted the bamboo poles removed. We took them out, and the sudden rush of stones and water still didn't happen. The tree went in, with a few more foot stomps onto the top of the bole. He quickly tossed soil around and began soaking the whole area with water, carrying the soil down around the roots.

When it was flooded, he paused, let the water sink, then piled on more soil and repeated the process.

Once the tree was in and the soil packed around its roots, he decided that I could probably handle the rest. He gave me instructions to repeat the process till the soil was up to there— he emphasized, pointing insistently, till I indicated with my finger on the narrow trunk of the tree where I was to stop piling soil. Fertilize next spring with 14-14-40, two spoonfuls only. I think. Then do that again a month later. Shoot water from hose up through the pine needles to release dead ones. And away they went. Leaving me to admire the handsome pine.

It is odd to be doing all this when some features of the aesthetic of Japanese gardens don't appeal to me at all. The problem with that statement is that it suggests there is a single graspable aesthetic. But I mean the kinds of things one sees in typical books about Japanese gardens. What does appeal, even though I don't think I can replicate it in any way, is the stark

The pine in place.

clear areas of crushed granite gravel, with well-placed dark stones, a few stately stands of sparse bamboo, and perhaps a couple of thoughtful ferns. There is a narrow line between the careful wabi-sabi refined elegance of casual unpressured naturalness and a simple mess; and the season's change, with untrained growth and autumn leaves, can easily carry one's garden across the line—unless one is there every day preserving the apparent randomness.

Between the bog and the pond

All that remained now was the irregular patch between the wall by the fence, the wall of the bog, the stream, and the pond. For the first time, I sat down with paper and actually began to plan this space. It would be what I would be looking down on from my desk in the teahouse, so I wanted to make it fairly typically Japanese in style. I had already put in a couple of privet bushes next to the ascending hose from the pump into the bog, with the reasonable expectation that they would grow and cover the hose within a year or so. As I made notes, there seemed endless possibilities for this small space, but I was struck by a phrase in one of the books I had read. The author suggests that the design is completed when there is nothing more that can be *removed* from the garden.

As I sat there sketching what might be done, I decided first that I should make the line of large basalt stones that flanked the stream less obtrusive. They looked too military, overseeing the small stream like stern guards. I began by removing the big stones from the side I was now going to shape, and in their place put smaller stones gathered from earlier excavations and from a bit of further harvesting from around the garden. Among those, to make sure the liner was completely covered, I sprinkled more drain pebbles. To support the steep slope from the edge of the stream down to the level of the area to be developed, I built in four or five of the larger rocks that

Stones by the stream from the bog to the pond—needing a bit more order. The tip of Moby Rock is in the right forefront.

were still looking for a home and a use. The plan called for small ferns across the top of the rocks, a mix of hardy, low-growing evergreens, and taller delicate maidenhairs that will move lightly through the summer.

My sketch called for a maple, a rounded mugo pine, some stones, possibly a patch of moss around the base of the maple. I also wanted a largish patch of heather, in memory of my Scottish mother. And some mondo grass that might grow over the harsh stones at the edge of the pond.

After this bout of heroic and unaccustomed planning, which was in lieu of my usual blundering forward and improvising on the basis of the blunders, I had the great idea of actually going out to measure the space I had available. Another sobering experience. Sketched on a large piece of paper, with blobs for plants and stones, there seemed a lot of room. Finding that the space is only seven feet long by about two feet at its narrowest and five feet at its widest made some of my expectations seem a tad ambitious.

The plan also didn't manage to survive a visit to the nursery.

I found some attractive ground cover that looks like miniature green and purple ferns, called Black Brass-Buttons (*Cotula* 'Platt's'). I got six pots, and then added six pots of purple heather, a drooping small maple, a mugo pine, and various ferns.

During the afternoon I put in the maple and mugo pine and then began adding the ground cover below the maple, and set the heather along the line of stones by the pond. I watered profusely and watched the brown soil-runoff dribble into the pond — despite the extra bits of liner I had put in there and the drain-tile stones I had buried to carry the water into the soil behind the liner. In my frenzy of planting, I had raised the level of the soil around the heather too high.

I looked at it all and felt depressed. In part, I was depressed that I would have to try to add more liner to keep runoff water from carrying soil into the pond. But also, the small raised garden was beginning to look like any kind of garden. It had nothing distinctively Japanese about it.

In bed, I realized I could solve both problems at once. I needed to lower the level of the ground between the maple and the pond, so the water would drain away into the soil and

Liner and stones to protect the pond from garden overflow.

not slurp into the pond, and also take out the long row of heather. I decided to keep one heather for my mother's sake and to build a small bamboo fence, about six inches to a foot high, that would curve across the seven-foot length of the raised garden. The three big stones that had been flopped around waiting to be moved yet again into a final place would be incorporated into the bamboo fence, creating a two-tiered garden. The lower tier I could cover with gravel or coarse sand, and the higher terrace would hold the maple, the mat of Black Brass-Buttons, the ferns, and whatever else.

First I had to get bamboo. I imagined those thick poles, which I would cut up and drive into the ground to form the low wall. Back to the landscape supply yard, where the laconic manager seemed relatively cheerful to see me. I described what I wanted, and he sent me over to the shed where some time ago I had got the pond liner. I wanted irregularly sized pieces of bamboo and asked the young man on duty there for one twelve-foot pole six inches in diameter and two three-inch poles. The thickest poles were stacked behind a pallet of something covered with a blue tarp. The young man sighed.

"I'll have to get a forklift to move that."

"Okay. I'll go back to the office and pay, now that we've decided what I need."

Back at the office, the manager said that he thought the six-inch would be too big for what I had described. Also, he pointed out, the bamboo was like any tree, and tapered toward the top, so by putting top and bottom pieces side by side I would get the irregularity I was looking for. I could pay later but now needed to go back and stop the young man from using the fork-lift to get at the biggest bamboo that I no longer wanted. Too late, of course. When I got back, he had moved the pallet and unstitched one of the burlap bags they were packed in, and, I assumed from his heavy breathing, had had to struggle to pull one out for me. How to tell him delicately that I didn't want it?

"Will you hate me forever and run the forklift into my car if I mention that I should stick to the two- or three-inch poles?"

He just sighed and even managed a little smile, pulled out three of the narrower poles, each twelve feet long, and grunted as he heaved the six-incher back into its sacking.

"How are you going to carry them?"

"I thought I'd open the back window of the passenger side of the car, and slide them over the seat to the front. That'll leave six feet hanging out."

He sighed again.

"I'll cut them in half for you."

I had expected an electric saw that would take care of the job in seconds, but he rooted around on a cluttered bench and came back with a rather delicate-looking pruning saw that had clearly seen better days. He bent to the cutting with energy, the saw occasionally buckling under the pressure. I was able to pack the six pieces through the passenger rear window, and he acknowledged my thanks with a sigh-full wave and wishes of good luck with building the bamboo wall.

When I returned to the office to pay, the manager measured the diameter of the poles, while I pointed out that they were a lot thinner at one end than another. He seemed to reach a generous compromise, calling them two inches. I said I wanted to put gravel up against them, but wondered whether the huge heap I had just walked by in the yard wasn't a bit too somber a gray. I asked if I could take a handful to see what it might look like when I had the bamboo fence up. He reached back for a large and sturdy plastic bag.

"Take what you want. Don't worry."

Back home, I cut the bamboo at an angle into sections from about nine inches to two feet long. The angle was to provide a point to make driving them into the ground easier. It took a little time to hammer them in. Great skill is required to achieve the ideal irregularity such a wall requires. One doesn't want the bamboo all the same size, uniformly stacked one against the other. However hard I might try to make the bamboo trim and neat, it leaned one way or the other. But, as I looked at it, I thought it had an attractive irregularity that a kindly priest at an obscure temple might not find so terrible. I rolled the remaining three large stones to slot into the curving line of the wall. Then I dug out the soil on the pond side and tossed it behind my new wall, and, lo, there was a neat little terrace.

Hammering the bamboo was like striking a chunk of metal. I began by laying a piece of wood over the top in order not to damage the rim of the bamboo as I drove it into the ground. But the wood began crumbling to pulp, and I took to hammering the bamboo directly. No plant has so many and varied uses. In the East, it is often used instead of steel rods to strengthen concrete. The hollow woody culms are segmented by septa, or nodes, that give it remarkable strength combined with lightness. I remember being surprised on my first visit to Hong Kong to see vast towers sheathed by bamboo scaffolding and being more surprised to discover that they survived hurricanes that smashed Western metal scaffolds. Tapping the widest part of the coppery green culm with a hammer gives a dull, flat bell-like sound. The combination called to mind Liu Changqing's poem:

> From the temple, deep in its tender bamboos,
> Comes the low sound of an evening bell,
> While the hat of a pilgrim carries the sunset
> Farther and farther down the green mountain.
> (*translated by Witter Bynner*)

My small terrace was something less than mountain scale, but the levels up from the pond, to the lower terrace, to the higher terrace, and then the basalt stones that support the bog suggest, to the fertile imagination, the sides of a mountain.

The problem now was what to put on the lower level. I needed to build it up a bit first. I still had about three-quarters of a bag of those round, tan-colored hydroponic clay marbles left over from building the bog. I thought I could make a base of those, put some landscaping fabric on top of them, and then either stones or gravel or coarse sand. The tan marbles looked pretty good by themselves, till I stood on them. Instead of crushing down, they took off in all directions as soon as I put my weight on them. I nearly took off into the pond as well. No doubt they felt quite reasonable behaving like a mass of firm round marbles, but I hadn't expected them to be quite so skittish. Even with fabric and stones on top, this was too unstable a base, and I would need to stand on it sometimes to get at the garden in the higher part of the terrace. So I scooped them out again. In one half of the space, I spread the pea-gravel I had got from the landscape supply center, and in the other half I emptied a bag of the granite gravel I had been putting in the tops of the marginal plants.

As I pondered which kind of gravel should win, my wife came out. I asked her opinion. If we agreed on the darker pea-gravel, then I could finish there and then, as I had enough to complete the job. If we chose lighter and larger granite chunks then I would have a long trip to the nursery which carries that particular kind. Yes, of course, we both agreed that the granite was better.

Now what was I going to put on the top level of the terrace behind the bamboo minifence? The thing I like most in the garden is the moss. It is restful, retains its rich color through the year, is undemanding and unfussy, and is as happy as a spore in acidic soil in this climate. Maybe I am overdoing the moss? But this terrace is narrow, will be entirely in the shade, and should contrast with the lighter granite gravel below. I had managed to supply myself with significant quantities of moss (as described in Chapter 6), by prevailing on neighbors who were in general only too happy to let me relieve them of their rich islands of the stuff. (The Brass-Buttons were less attractive than the moss, so I put them around the base of the pine.)

In a local nursery, I found a few small Korean rock ferns, in a scraggy pile of almost discarded pots of bits and pieces left over from last year. They still insisted on full price, even though the poor things looked entirely neglected and one was somewhat withered, but it would no doubt perk up with spring. I also picked up a couple of deer ferns, and a fern whose pot had lost its label, which no one could identify. I put the rock ferns by the stream, and the bigger deer ferns to the left side of the

The finished bamboo-terraced area. The squat plant among the gravel is the mugo pine. The privets over to the left are beginning to work at hiding the pipe carrying water from the pond to be cleaned in the bog. The higher terrace is covered with star moss, with a couple of deer ferns in the middle, and a maple next to them. To the right, hanging over the bamboo that is supporting the terrace, is a single purple heather.

upper terrace across from the maple. Then it was simply a matter of fitting moss around the plants. I put the unidentified fern at the top point by the stream, close to the waterfall from the bog. A prominent spot. A bit risky, perhaps, but I would keep an eye on it.

I think I have managed to reduce the elements of the raised garden to a minimum. If I were to take away any item, it would be too stark, yet as it is, it has a simplicity and, dare I claim, a spare elegance; stones, moss, the bamboo fence, ferns, the squat mugo pine, the privets, and a small maple.

I bought a couple of bags of the granite gravel, spread it over the pea-gravel, and that's all I could do without the help of spring and summer. Once it warms up, I will put umbrella plants around the inner rim of the bog and set a carpet of water hyacinth into the surface gravel to do another summer's water cleaning and propagating, as only they know how.

The paving stones and fern border

Behind the wall of the
raised garden and in front of the shed and compost heap, the
grass—shaded by huge neighboring conifers—gets hardly any
sun. Strictly speaking, "grass" is not the right word. There was
some grass there once, and until recently maybe a few tough
and determined blades had continued to fight their way
through the blanket of weeds. But I had dumped stones on it
and later dragged them off again, cut and hammered wood on
it, spilled and then trod gravel into it, let discarded pond liner
sit on it, painted the fence boards over it, and used it as a park-
ing lot for the wheelbarrow, wood, and bags of stones. Now
the abused and scarred piece of ground had no vegetation at
all to show. It got its revenge by turning to mud in the rain.

I needed to pave this increasingly sad patch. But with what?
The books about Japanese gardening have many pictures of
stone paths. They are invariably of carefully laid stones of different sizes. Always in the set are some that must require Stonehenge building equipment and techniques to get into place. I
was restricted by what I could get through our narrow gate and
carry, or wheelbarrow, to the back of the garden. Also, the
stone-yards I went to were selling those enormous stones by

the pound, so a decent chunk of stone would take an indecent chunk from my bank account. And this wasn't a path—it didn't lead anywhere; it was just a bit of space in front of the compost heap. As my wife and I would be pushing the wheelbarrow to and from the compost heap for the next century or so, the surface I put down would need to be sturdy and level.

Well, I'm already beginning to protest too much. Setting aside all Japanese gardening rules, I decided to put down exposed-aggregate concrete 2' × 2' paving slabs, which are available at any lumberyard. I decided also to put 2" × 2" strips of wood between the large slabs and to stain the wood the same dark charcoal-black as the fence.

In a proper Japanese garden you would be careful to avoid the crude regular shapes that I was contemplating. And particularly you would not allow four corners to meet together. My paving stones would be a wretched concatenation of painful, unsightly right angles. The proper placement of stones is an ancient art. An eleventh-century gardening manual—the *Sakuteiki*—gives precise instructions for laying stones so that they will harmonize with each other and with the human soul. The author is not reticent about describing the catastrophes that will descend on careless rock placers. The tea ceremony masters of the sixteenth century developed this art in their construction of paths through tea gardens to the small building where the tea ceremony would take place. The purpose of these paths was to prepare the mind for the ceremony by inducing repose and calmness of spirit. The wandering asymmetry of the stones that constituted the paths suggests the asymmetries of nature, and the artist who created the garden would design its rambling course to provide varied viewpoints on its plants, stones, sand, water.

Since in Japanese mythology devils can walk only in straight lines, keeping to a curving or zigzag path would enable one to leave evil behind. The mythology supports a good aesthetic principle. But my paving stones would be an inviting smooth highway to whatever demons lurk around our neighborhood. At least I would be leading them from the condominium fence onto the lawn, or the reverse, so preventing them gamboling evilly, or whatever Japanese demons do, around the raised garden, pond, or teahouse. In mitigation of my sin, I declared this paved area to be outside the Zen garden proper.

Before one can do what one wants to get on with, one has to do other things, and before doing the other things . . . I couldn't start laying the stones until I had dug down and created a bed of compactible gravel, then put some landscape fabric on top of the gravel to prevent weeds coming up, and on top of that adding a layer of sand on which the pavers would sit. But I couldn't do any of *that*, I reluctantly concluded, till I had stained the bases of the compost heap and the shed. Their foundations would be under the finished surface level, and I wanted to give them the extra protection of staining. I decided to use the same solid-color stain that I had used on the fence, largely for the good Irish reason that I had a couple of cans still sitting there.

So I dug down around the bases of the compost heap and shed and stained what wood I could get at. The trouble with having a paintbrush in hand is that everything one sees needs painting. So I stained the whole of the compost heap container and went higher on the shed than I had intended, managing to stop myself at about door height because that's where I ran out of the green stain. Thus, for many months visitors could admire a partly stained shed, begun serendipitously and stopped in a fit of forgetfulness. If the paint had held out, the trees and stones would have been lucky to escape.

At this point I brought to bear on the job the mathematical expertise passed down from those ingenious ancient Greeks. If the pavers were two inches deep, and I needed to put down a further couple of inches or so of gravel, and a further inch or so of sand, the few inches I had excavated at great cost to my knees and back were derisorily inadequate. If I had begun pouring on gravel at that point, I would need to add a step to reach the surface of the pavers.

Now I proceeded to overdo it and went down to coal-mining depths. At least I bared all the posts of the shed and compost heap and was able to splash charcoal stain on them with abandon. Most of the time, one has to be careful not to drip when painting and to be minutely careful not to go over edges. Painting is too evocative of fear-filled primary school, with some ferocious battle-ax determined to further one's artistic career by threatening brimstone to anyone who did not keep religiously within the lines. But for a few minutes there was a glorious freedom in which dripping didn't matter, and everything paintable could be the same color—although the charcoal was also close to running out.

As I went farther down, I became only too aware of the number of surrounding trees, each of which had sent major delegations of roots to just where I was digging. It took ages hacking and cutting and heaving. I found the pruning shears effective on the smaller roots, and the larger succumbed to the merciless sharp-toothed ministrations of a dry-wall knife.

While slashing away the local trees' living access to food, and while damning their impossible sturdiness and writhing pursuit of every nutrient in the soil, one also must wonder at their enterprise and cunning. Once a tree's seed is fertilized, it first sends down a root to anchor itself to the earth. Our failure to do this has meant we can travel to Las Vegas or Wigan, but as a result, we are somewhat rootless wanderers on the surface of the planet. The root absorbs water and dissolved minerals from the ground and sucks them along its astonishing length and delivers them to the trunk of the tree, which then takes over and delivers them to the branches and leaves. In this small area I cleaved through some roots as thick as my wrist,

Effective tools: pruning shears and a dry-wall knife.

and pulled out miles of tiny, delicate, crinkly strands no thicker than a strand of wool. I could put a shovel in the ground almost anywhere in this suburb of Vancouver and hit the roots of some tree. The huge pine that blocks so much light from my Japanese garden has a mass of roots which, if cut and laid end to end, would stretch from here to . . . oh, to there. These ferocious roots provide us with so many metaphors. Most commonly we use the word to suggest the real basis of a thing, which encourages us to melancholy reflections on our own roots, tangled and spreading back in time to our birth, and then back through our begetters and their begetters. Well, before I lie down in this now neatly excavated slice of earth, dug deeper than it needed to be, I should get on with paving it.

Laying the pavers
The next step, after the back- and knee-breaking digging and cutting of roots, was to level the area with a bed of compactible gravel. This is easy work. I wheelbarrowed it from the same pile that I had used for the space around the bamboo and along

The compactible gravel somewhat compacted. The slope isn't as bad as it looks, due to the end 2" × 4" not being level.

the fence. Once the soil is covered, it is a simple matter, and quite pleasant, to rake it level. It fills the dips and irregularities in the soil below. One then goes around tamping it down to make it firm. At this point, one discovers, or creates, further irregularities, and so a bit more raking and tamping are called for. And then some more, and a bit more leveling, till one becomes absolutely fed up with this pleasant activity.

Buying the pavers proved embarrassing. I had priced them at the local lumberyards and the larger hardware stores. They ranged from something like $8 to $12 for the identical product. I preferred to buy them at our local hardware store, with its small yard and people I have known for twenty-five years, who have so graciously taken thousands of dollars off me in that time. Guess who wanted $12? The pavers would have to be delivered from wherever I bought them, as they were too heavy for my car. I was in the local store, and I needed sixteen of them, and thought I might as well pay the extra for the convenience of getting them ordered and delivered immediately. So I bellied up to the service counter and put in my order to the young woman from whom I had over the years bought paint, nails, hammers, ladders, glue, and received endless tips about using them. As we chatted while she made out the bill, I mentioned that one of the megastores was selling them for $4 less. I had meant this as a piece of information, expecting that she might smilingly commiserate as she took my credit card.

"How much?" she asked.

"I think it was $7.89."

She stopped writing and looked quite solemn for a moment. I thought perhaps I'd offended her.

"I'll get the manager," she said as she sped off to the rear.

Oh no. She assumed I was bargaining, which I suppose any sensible person might. But if I'd wanted the cheaper price, I'd have gone to the place offering it.

The manager came back with her, both looking grim. I feared I might be in for a tough bargaining response, or even a Monty Pythonish tearful account of his impoverished children and how the business was on the verge of going under and this could be the demand that brought the place to its knees. Mind you, I knew that his children were more likely howling for BMWs and wide-screen home theaters, and that he drove one of those upmarket SUVs.

He twirled the computer screen around, and pointed at a list of numbers I couldn't make any sense of.

"Our wholesale price for the pavers is $7.22 each. See there. And that's what our competitors are paying too. It must be a major sale item over there. Selling them at $7.89 is hardly worth our while getting them in." He was a handsome man, whom I had seen on my irregular visits to the store for the past quarter century. He had been a schoolboy working weekends for his father when I first remembered seeing him, and now he was a serious and honorable citizen. I've no idea what has happened to the father. Perhaps I helped in my small way toward his early retirement in Palm Springs or Hawaii.

I tried to indicate agreement that no reasonable person could expect him to sell the pavers for the pathetic amount his competitor was satisfied to accept. How considerate of him to be offering them, almost giving them away, for merely $12 each. Perhaps he was being too generous? But he was too busy ruminating to notice my compliance.

"But if that's what they are letting them go for, we can't have our customers disadvantaged." He smiled, a decisive, rather sad smile, I thought, and authorized the young woman to let me have them for $7.89. The worst part was the way she looked at me, the kind of accusatory look appropriately directed at a carpetbagger brutally stripping assets from a helpless widow. It was one of those disappointed but nevertheless satisfied looks that suggested her low opinion of human nature, or perhaps just customers, was being confirmed yet again. Telling her I wasn't trying to bargain seemed too little too late. The damage was done, and the business would no doubt come crumbling in my callous wake.

The next stage was laying the landscaping fabric, which would discourage any weeds that might try to push through the gravel. Given how deep I had dug, and consequently how much gravel I had to put on to get back near the earth's surface, it seemed unlikely that anything could hope to grow through, even my bamboo should they manage a breakout from their water barriers. But the landscape fabric is cheap, and a layer wouldn't do any harm. One lays it down, overlapping by about six inches as one goes, to make life difficult for any unusually persistent weed. But what other kind of weed is there but the persistent type? I know I am going to put huge and heavy blocks of concrete on top of all this, but I have seen weeds peeping along the cracks of this kind of paver.

One of the small disasters was my assumption that the two-inch dimension of a 2" × 2" would be the same as that of the two-inch-deep concrete pavers. Not so. There is a good quarter inch or so difference; in the case of the wood, 2" × 2" are the dimensions before it is milled smooth. This was a problem because the paving stones are thus deeper than the 2" × 2"s. And this meant that once the pavers were laid around the 2" × 2"s, I would have to lever out each piece of wood and pour in, very carefully, just the right amount of sand to bring it to the same level as the paving stones. I'm sure my character was improved by this time-consuming and meticulous activity, as was my acquaintance with the remarkable qualities of sand.

Pouring the sand from the bags didn't help my delicate knees. (Four knee operations and counting.) But I emptied all the bags, hoping I had enough sand for the job. There was a hint of Zen-master work when I carefully scraped a piece of wood over the 2" × 2" guide strips I had laid on the landscaping fabric. I went to and fro till the sand was pretty evenly spread across the whole area. Most of this sand is probably the pounded residue of quartz, which is hard, nearly insoluble in water, and will not decompose. Letting a dry handful drain through fingers is a curious sensation that nearly all of us have experienced. One sees children do it again and again. There are so many individual grains: a metaphor for numerousness. They spill like the seconds of our lives: so many, yet all gone so quickly. Fine sand pours almost like a liquid and conveniently adapts to our shape on the beach, but also provides just the right amount of resistance. Clearly, evolution intended us to lie on beaches.

The sand needed wetting and tamping down, to make it firm and flat. Once that was done, we could begin laying the pavers. These monsters are pretty heavy. I managed to coopt one of my sons and a friend of his who was visiting from

The sand layer.

Ireland. I don't think the friend had imagined his Canadian holiday would involve heaving around paving stones, but he leaned into it with a will.

In a few cases, once the paver was down, it was clear that the sand underneath was uneven because the paver rocked up

Laying the pavers. Note the soccer-generated calves on my son.

and down when one stood on it and moved one's weight from side to side. Correcting this problem required the increasingly less willing helpers to hoist it out again, being careful not to disturb the sand in the process. I was doing my best to be the jolly foreman while they did the hard work, and I tried not to groan and suck breath through my teeth too quickly whenever they dragged a chunk of sand out of place while hoisting up a heavy paver, or laid one corner down hard before the others, creating further unevenness. It was a delicate matter; they were noble volunteers, and the initial unevennesses were my fault, but if they were able to put the slabs down flat, everything would be easier. Once a slab had to be raised up again, they then had to hold it ready as I dived in with fistfuls of sand, building up the low areas, shaving the high areas, and tamping down both. Sometimes the movement in the slab was just a little, and due to a lack of firmness in the sand at the front. In such cases I simply shoved as much sand as I could force under the slab with my fingers. Our son enjoyed calling this, rather impiously, my Zen-master technique.

The paving stones ready for feet.

Dribbling the right amount of sand into the slots where the 2" × 2"s were to sit proved easier than I had expected. With a little help from my friends, we soon had all the pavers in place. The last, smaller set—one foot by two feet—fitted not quite neatly beside the compost heap, and I then needed just a single one-foot-by-one-foot slab for the top corner.

The one-foot slabs at the side still left a few inches in front of the compost heap. I had thought of cutting a piece of wood to fit, and then staining it black. But the front of the compost heap was not exactly square with the pavers, though the pavers were square with the front of the shed. The perfect solution, or at least an adequate one, was to use the colored stones I had bought to try as samples against the fence. There were just enough to fill the space. I suspect that the only really perfect features of this garden have come about through chance like this. Story of our lives?

The purple and green stones at the edge of the path, against the compost heap.

With the sturdy pavers in place, I had an area of soil about a foot wide between their edge and the raised-garden wall. What should I put there? While I thought about this, I had to bring that excavated area up to the level of the pavers. I set about this with extreme care, taking spadefuls from the compost heap and trying not to let any grains fall on the handsome pavers, with their now smartly painted dignified black spacers. I failed, of course, as bits kept falling from the spade. When finished, I brushed away every speck of dirt, wondering how long I was likely to keep that degree of cleanliness up.

A fern border

An obvious contender for the patch of shady soil was ferns. The hunt began. I'm sure James Bond hasn't spent many afternoons wandering around nurseries looking for just the right kind of fern for a stretch of earth that measures fifteen feet by one foot. But it is an adventure of a kind. You will perhaps be unsurprised by now to discover that there are over 10,000 known species of ferns. I suppose they say "known" because one might any day wade into new species in the Amazon basin or downtown Philadelphia. The Amazon Indians no doubt "know" those ferns, but the Indians are clearly not who the textbooks have in mind when they say the ferns are unknown. I can't say I checked out all of the species, but among this magnificent diversity there are tiny Ophioglossales (and, yes, it will be on the test later), which put up a single tiny frond a year, and enormous Cyatheae, which have trunks as much as eighty feet tall, capped with a luxuriant crown of fronds. It seems that ferns were the most prominent form of plant on the planet during the Carboniferous period, just before my first knee operation, around 260,000,000 years ago. These massive fern forests are in significant part responsible for the Earth's coal beds.

This satisfying accumulation of knowledge didn't actually help me to make a choice among the varieties available in our local post-Carboniferous nurseries. I eliminated many species by wanting evergreen varieties. In our local forests there are some heartstoppingly lovely maidenhair ferns, but they fade away during the winter months. In the end, in the small nursery where I got the black bamboo, I found four pots of deer ferns. These are evergreen and generously multiarmed. One of the ferns was squashed, though. I contemplated buying only three, thinking the fourth might be too damaged to grow successfully. The guy who had been perfunctorily helping me seemed unperturbed when I pointed out the smashed fern.

"Oh, yes. I dropped a hosta on it the other day."

He poked at the broken and battered stems for a minute.

"It'll be okay next year," he said, handing it back to me. No word of having it for half price, and his words were accompanied by halitosis of heroic proportions, through which I would have to pass if I were to put the fern down again. It seemed better to take it, and wait for its resurrection next year.

I planted them in the border, giving special care to the victim of the crushing hosta. Again, neat regularity of spacing is inappropriate for a Japanese garden. Even so, I put them in line, having little alternative, assuming the regularity would appear less so as they grew.

Another pine and more moss

But there was still a space at the front corner by the curve of the wall. I tried a variety of plants—a tumbling evergreen Mexican grass, a couple of different shrubs—but nothing seemed to work. After the success of the black pine up by the bog, I thought another might do the trick; a smaller, slimmer one that would echo but not echo, and balance but not balance the pine above. I went back to the nursery one Saturday afternoon in January.

I got out of the car a little warily, fearing that the samurai might be around. I wanted to look at the trees at leisure, and feared that he would descend on me like a force of nature and insist on what I needed, carrying his chosen plants and me and tossing us all into the car. Fortunately, the younger man whom I had met on my first visit (the son of the silent sage) ambled out of the shed when he saw me wandering among his set of pines. He stood back for a while and later agreed that the slim one would fit in the space I had, and that I could probably get it into the back of my car. But not today. It is too cold, he said.

"Another few . . ." He felt the air, rubbing it between his fingers, unable to find the word. "Warm. Too cold now. Only a few . . ."

"A few degrees warmer?"

"Degrees. Yes. A few. You come back when it is degrees warmer."

"Should I leave a deposit?"

He laughed as though this was a great joke.

"I put a ribbon on it. You come when you want. You bought the other. I know you."

We bowed to each other.

A week later I turned up and we decided that my new pine wouldn't fit in the car after all. The delivery next morning involved the samurai who had slammed the first pine in place. I had dug a hole ready for it, putting the soil on an old shower curtain on the lawn. The samurai inspected the hole and laughed.

"Hole too small again. Dig more out here, and here!"

I dug. More! The anorexic youth was with him and took over from me. We discussed how it should sit, and this time I spent the extra minute thinking and it was slotted into space. There was much friendly discussion of the weather and fertilizing, and we parted cheerfully.

But it looked a tad stark. What it needed, I decided, was a moss base. Time to go hunting again. I scavenged around the garden, grateful that the moss had been energetically propagating itself since my last foray. But even so, I didn't have enough. Desperate measures were called for.

The smaller pine in moss, with a clump of heather.

I phoned a friend who lives a few blocks away and confessed I had a rather odd request. After getting beyond the difficulty of her thinking that I was asking if I could have any moths she didn't want, she was quite eager for me to come and alleviate her decades-long battle against moss. She said she had acres of the stuff. And indeed she had, and large rich pads of just the right variety. Her daughter and two granddaughters were visiting, so my salivating eagerness to get my spade under the loads of moss that had been their despair for years made the visit something of a minor party for a few minutes. The children were too polite to ask why this man was piling large chunks of grandma's garden into the back of his car.

Filling in the area around the base of the new pine with the moss produced a humped and irregular green mound. While irregular, it seemed too smooth, so I added a small Korean rock fern among the moss on one side, and a clump of heather on the other, and decided that I had, for now, finished the paved area between the wall and the compost heap.

seven

Framing the teahouse/study

I MENTIONED EARLIER THE influences that flowed from Chinese artists' huts in the mountains to the creation of the Japanese teahouse and that my purpose was more akin to the Chinese retreat for study and work than the contemplative, austere, and ceremonial Japanese teahouse. But the Western idea of the study also influences my plans—if plans they can be called. While the secluded hut of China was converting into the urban garden teahouse of Japan, in Europe something not entirely different in spirit was taking place. In the medieval house, all rooms, including the bedrooms, were public spaces. The modern idea of privacy seems to have been a later development. But during the Renaissance in Italy a distinct kind of room was invented. The *studio* was a small private room set off for "studious leisure."

In the studio the owner could read and write or reflect on life with the help of favorite classical authors, whose works were becoming more available. Possibly the monastic cell provided a model for the rich man's study—a private place of contemplation, study, and prayer. Or so Dora Thornton suggests in *The Scholar in His Study* (New Haven: Yale University Press, 1998).

A degree of ceremony and reverence for the activities in such rooms was not uncommon, as developed in the East with the teahouse. Machiavelli, heeding the advice I ignored of the master gardener—that distinctive clothing is appropriate for any task one wishes to undertake in the right spirit—solemnly changed clothing before entering his study to commune with the ancient, mighty dead.

These earliest Western studies were typically furnished sparsely with a built-in desk and bench. A revolving lectern might be present. There would also be a few shelves for books or antique ornaments. This I will likely replicate, putting out there my Roman oil lamps and small vases, and perhaps the ancient Greek bronze spearheads I had bought—much corroded, so I got them very cheap. They had been found in Asia Minor and dated to around 1200 B.C., so one of them might have been the one that got Achilles in the heel.

As time went by, the decoration and furniture of the studio became more elaborate. Trust a Medici (Piero, in this case) to have a vaulted ceiling inlaid with roundels—those decorative carved medallions—by Luca della Robbia, representing the Labors of the Months. Not something I expect to emulate. Just can't find that quality of labor around here for some reason. But even if one could, and could afford it, the Japanese (and early European) ideal of simplicity and a certain starkness attracts me.

The starkness or sparseness of physical surroundings is a reflection of the lack of clutter one desires for the mind. So the teahouse is to be a retreat from the crowding cares and huggermugger of daily life, from its newspapers, radios, and TVs, and from the clamor that is so hard to shake from one's mind. Nan-jung Chu visited the Taoist sage Lao Tzu. As the man approached, Lao Tzu said, "Why did you come with all this crowd of people?" Surprised, Nan-jung Chu whirled around, but saw no one. It was his baggage of anxieties, the clutter of voices in his mind, and his everyday concerns the sage observed in him. So as we approach the teahouse, we are to leave our crowds behind; we are to go in alone, as we were born alone and shall die alone, whatever crowds may be around us.

Beginning the teahouse

The path to this serene and simple place is through a lot of work, sweat, dirt, ruined clothes and boots, damaged fingers, bruised legs, strained back, pulled muscles, cuts and lacerations, aching knees, shoulders, and elbows, endless silent and not so silent cursing, significant anxiety about costs, shouted frustrations at stupid errors, and much else that seems to share little with the end in view.

But as I begin building, I realize my lack of planning has reached pathological proportions; I have no idea what I am going to do. I imagine I would like to have an Asian-style roof, with wide overhangs, though I have no idea how to build such things. They are not common on the more simple teahouse styles I have seen, and aren't standard bits one can pick up at the local lumberyards. One thing at a time; just set about doing the next thing, and bit by bit it will just happen.

I don't even know whether to build it on stilts or lay a concrete pad at ground level. I have vaguely imagined a raised teahouse, with a few steps going up to it and a narrow veranda under the long curving roof that juts out over the pond. Why should I build it above ground? Why not? *Is* it a memory of the Swiss Family Robinson, contented in their tree house? It's not the most practical way to go, but if practicality is the criterion that is supposed to dominate here, I'd never have done any of this. Perhaps it is an image of sitting on a balcony or veranda raised a little above the pond, from which one could look down and feed the fish or watch the waterfall.

The area left for the teahouse is where I had been tossing all the rubble and waste soil I couldn't work out what to do with earlier. First I would have to get rid of the now grassy mound of mixed clay and topsoil I had been chasing round the garden from the time I began on the fence.

Most of what was here, though, came out of what is now the pond. I began digging into the mound, thinking I was so familiar with this particular pile it might start calling me by my first name. There was space for some of it, perhaps all of it, to the rear of the shrubs on the north side of the garden. Just to make life difficult, I seemed to have sprung a leak in the tire on the wheelbarrow, so carting the soil away had to wait on getting a bicycle pump. Then it was slow work, spading the soil into the wheelbarrow, then taking it ten yards or so down the garden, looking for places behind the shrubs that might be able to accommodate wandering loads of mostly infertile soil. A few afternoons of hefting and slinging got rid of the whole pile. Then I gathered up the leftover acreage of liner and found a place for it under the back deck of our house, piled against the shed bits of wood from earlier building, and I tossed against the north fence the dozens of stones that had been dug out of the excavations.

Then I raked and weeded until I had a smooth and neat piece of teahouse-sized real estate. I think it is this stage that gives me most satisfaction, like looking down at the sculpted space for the pond, or the shaped stream bed from the bog. At this point it was tempting to decide that what I needed there was just a raked piece of dark brown soil. Well, not very tempting perhaps.

The next trick was to work out how big I would make the teahouse, and what shape it would be, and where I would put the support posts—little things like that. The kind of things it is good to sort out before getting too advanced, lest one try building teahouses in the sky. If I used up all the space, I could build it about ten feet deep, with a two-foot jog halfway along the back wall to avoid the cedar tree that my wife is reluctant

Here's the space for the teahouse, after I move that pile of clayey soil. The chicken-wire frames that protect the pond overnight are against the fence.

to lose. I thought that could create an attractive alcove inside, with tall, narrow windows on one or both sides of it, and a seat in the base, cushioned; a nice place for reading. There seemed room for about twelve feet across the front. So I began pegging it out.

It quickly became clear that using up the whole space was not a good idea. It would push the teahouse right up against two sets of the bamboo, leaving no room to get around the back. Also I thought I would have to forgo my alcove, as according to our city bylaws, I needed to leave three feet from the neighbor's fence. So I was reduced to a simple eight-by-ten-foot space. I pegged it out roughly, tied string around the pegs where the walls would be, and put a garden chair in the middle to get a sense of the space I would have. It was enough for a small writing surface and a chair.

The cleared site for the teahouse/study is to the left, roughly staked out.

I bought the wood I needed to build the posts and to string joists between them and lay a plywood floor on top. Once the base was in place, I would begin the framing—but I'd put off planning that until the base was finished, on the assumption that what I did there would reduce considerably the options I then had, which would in turn reduce the need to plan.

So first I would need to dig the holes into which I would put the posts that would support the raised teahouse. I went to rent the posthole digger that I had become familiar with when building the fence.

"How many holes?" asked the cheery equipment rental guy.

"Twelve."

"You'll want a power auger then. Much quicker, and twelve will take you ages with the hand digger."

I realized that, in all the times I had been there, he had

never rented me what I asked for. If I was always guided to something more expensive, I would recognize an easy pattern. But sometimes he insisted I needed a cheaper tool or would be better off with something I already had—like the time he wouldn't rent me a chain saw to get rid of a tree stump, insisting I use an ax. Good exercise, but a bit more wearing on the joints. A more complex psychological explanation was needed. It was as though this was his way of insisting on his professional status and my amateur incompetence. It's certainly not that I *always* asked for the wrong thing.

The auger required two people, and I wouldn't be able to get any help before the next weekend, so I thought I finally had him trapped. He would have to rent me the manual posthole digger I had come in for. But, no; he had a new kind of manual digger that he was sure I'd find better than the old one, and he insisted I give it a try.

The new one worked on a corkscrew principle. It had, at about waist height, a straight piece of wood across the top with handgrips on either end, like an upright bicycle's handlebars. The business end was like two narrow spades joined rigidly together, with a kind of cutting piece sticking out. The effect was that if one pushed down on the wide handles and turned, one would cut and loosen the soil, which would be dragged between the spadelike blades. Then one pulled up and threw the soil to one side. I began; push down and turn, and turn again, and again. After some time a small amount of soil fell between the two blades. Lift and toss aside. Then again, and again. This was hard and slow work. As soon as it encountered a stone or root, it shied off sideways, so I had to get a trowel or pruning shears and dig or cut out whatever was obstructing progress downward. Quite wearying, and mostly it didn't pull up the soil well. The soil dribbled over its sides, so I had to lean down and scoop it out by hand.

Eventually I was down about two feet, leaning in to scoop

out the loosened soil, and then I stopped, my nose inches from the top of the hole. What was the smell? Not just the mix of soil odors, from the top rich layer and the lower clay, and a wisp of something damp and fresh from the cut roots, but also something else, faint, like a ghost vanishing as I tried to capture it. Some animal smell. Something that died here a thousand years ago? It had a ghostly suspiration to it. Perhaps the last desperate exhalation of a caught skunk, held in the soil for decades or centuries till released just now. I'm sure smells can't last like that, nor was it so distinctively skunklike, but that's what came to mind, as something that clings tenaciously. And it was only the faintest half-caught smell, like an echo of something fading and hardly there, but yet undeniably there, a presence of some other form of life, disturbed.

I paused, looking into the shadowed hole, half expecting a whispered voice from the deep backward and abysm of time. What would it say? "You too will join us soon"? One hardly needs ghostly voices from the depths to deliver such banal messages. More likely, instead of such solemnities, the voice would be preceded by a few clicks and would ask in a bored tone for the expiration date of my credit card.

I sniffed at the other holes as I dug them out, but didn't again sense that curious faint animal odor. I was reminded of the Sufi teacher Ansari's words: "I heard a voice whispering in the night saying, 'There is no voice whispering in the night.'" The elusive ambivalence was like the reply of the old woman in the west of Ireland who was asked by an anthropologist whether she believed in fairies: "Indeed I do *not*, sir," she replied. "But they're there all the same."

At about two feet down in the third hole I hit another stone. I got out the trowel, and began trying to loosen it. After a few minutes scraping, I was certain that I had hit the head of Moby Rock's sibling. So that post would go down two feet, and no farther.

I spent a couple of hours, screwing the posthole digger down an inch or so at a time. It wasn't so bad when I was going through clear soil, but even a small stone or root had me again down with the trowel or pruning shears, hacking and cutting then pulling it out with my gloved hand. The glove was some protection, but as I pulled upward, soil from the sides of the hole dribbled down till my fingers were packed with soil inside and outside the glove. And my hand was increasingly sweaty, so the soil inside smeared and caked in the most attractive way. Occasionally, I expected a hand to come up and shake mine reaching down.

A couple of hours the next day, and then our elder son visited on the Sunday, and he had a go as well. After all this effort, I still didn't have half of them done. I needed mechanized violence.

I phoned Geoff, who had helped me get Moby Rock out of the pond area. He would be happy to help, and came over the next afternoon. I rented a power auger and we got it back home and into the garden. There were four handles sticking out at the top, with a broad metal screw at the business end, and an accelerator trigger on one handle. One pulled the starting handle and the gas engine burst into life.

It made an incredible racket, but dived downward into the soil as though taking a bite out of its favorite dessert after having not eaten for a week. It bored into the ground, but then got stuck. We realized that the trick was to let it bore down a few inches, then raise it so the soil caught in the screw would get thrown clear of the hole. We got into the pattern, and all seemed to go quite well, until the screw hit a root or stone. Once that happened, the auger would lurch to one side but continue its impressive chewing downward. In one or two cases, it hit something just under the surface, and veered off. After a while, I couldn't tell whether we had drilled holes in the right places or whether they had all shot off to undesired compass points. Geoff and I felt like marionettes pulled to and fro by this roaring demon whose sole aim seemed to be reaching Australia by the most direct route. But within an hour or so we had the remaining holes dug. We returned the auger to the rental shop with a small swagger to suggest we had managed to work the beast successfully, rather than admit that it worked us.

Putting in the supporting posts

I now faced the problem of getting the twelve posts all lined up and square. After dropping a few inches of small stones into each hole, to help drain water from the base of the posts underground, and pounding the stones with the post, I dropped a five-foot 4" × 4" into each hole, and felt some apprehension at the result. They didn't look much in line, nor did the whole thing look very square. I had only an hour or so in the evening of a couple of days the next week and it seemed as though I was making no progress at all in getting the posts the right distance from each other, each vertical, each in line, and all square. I had bought a number of ten-foot strips of 1" × 2" pieces of wood, and had been staking the posts in place, and then fastening them together with the long strips, which were supposed to hold them upright and in precise line. I knew the 3-4-5 method, derived from Pythagoras's theorem (i.e., measuring three feet on one side and four feet on the other, the diagonal across will be exactly five feet), but there just seemed too many dimensions to keep under control: I had to have them vertical, north-south and east-west, then in line with the posts running north-south, and with those running east-west, and all square. Well, I know I am overdoing this — if I had measured more carefully in the first place and controlled the auger better, it shouldn't have been such a problem. But I hadn't and it was.

The family next door to the south was having some renovations done. As I went out each morning to take the chicken-wire cover off the pond, I would chat with the carpenter. When I was home in my study I had seen him working during the day, measuring with great care, cutting with calm precision; he seemed a true craftsman. I asked him if he knew a way to get the base squared off easily.

"Yes. I'll come," he said, putting down his circular saw. A slight Dutch accent, kindly face, gray mustache.

He looked at my posts and ribbons of thin strips trying to hold them together and in place.

"It ought to be easier, I know," I said apologetically.

"Yes. It is easy. You see, take these three posts, this line," he said, pointing to the three parallel to my Japanese fence. "Put them right, then pour concrete. When that is dry, you have secure baseline. Then across there, and across there. It is easy. Measure three-four-five. There."

He smiled and waved as he wandered down the garden. Pardon? Could we go over that a few more times?

Well, at the very least he had given me the good idea to start with one line that is sure, and then concrete those three posts in place, and that was something to begin with. Which was better than constantly chasing my errors from one corner to another, trying to keep all the posts vertical, square, and in line. Each time I had fixed one post, it seemed to throw at least one of the others out in at least one dimension. So I started by firmly setting up the three posts, making sure they were vertical in all dimensions, in line with each other, and each precisely equidistant from the fence. I cut small stakes and pounded them into the ground, then nailed them to the 4" × 4"s, to make them entirely secure.

Then to mixing concrete. I was going to rent one of those mechanical jobs, but having been persuaded to put a few posts in at a time, I thought I might as well do the old mixing-in-the-wheelbarrow routine. I found indeed that it was much easier with a hoe than a shovel, and after a while I was ready to slurp the gray soup into the hole.

Concrete dries to a rather boring light gray, but when it is newly mixed and poured and first sets, it is a distinguished and serious dark shade, with hints of deeper greens or blues. Set around the first posts when I came out the next day, it seemed dignified and proud in its magic of turning from that slurped porridge to immovable servant.

By the end of a couple of hours of careful measurements and staking, I had the three end posts in place and embedded in concrete. A couple of days later I went out to do some more. Instead of doing the 3-4-5 measuring, as the craftsman working next door and every book in the land had told me, I decided to repeat what I had already done by measuring the four posts along the rear from the north fence. It was a bit difficult getting everything lined up, and some of the holes needed to be extended northward a few inches. So I troweled down, scooping the soil up by hand every few minutes, grainy clay gathering inside my glove as I worked. When all was in place, I mixed concrete and poured. After more precise measuring and staking, mixing and slurping, I finished the afternoon with three further posts embedded in concrete.

Put like that, it might seem that the concrete mixing was pretty easy. It involved the usual back-pulling work to get the water and gray powder and stones to mingle properly, and then more back and knee straining to add further mix to get the right consistency, and some cursing as I had to open another bag because I had put in too much water, and then adding a bit more water because I had put in too much mix, and so on. And while I had been digging out all those holes I had to deposit the soil somewhere. So the surface was unevenly mounded between the holes, like miniature Alps, and the wheelbarrow had to be maneuvered carefully to sit more or less level, but then had to be further maneuvered over the

The "immovable servant," concrete, around the first three posts.

Alps to be able to pour the concrete accurately into the holes. One time my sloppy working surface led to near disaster, as I was heaving the full barrow of ready-to-pour concrete over a hump, and it began to tumble sideways. They say one should let a barrow fall in such circumstances, as it is easy to do real damage to muscle, bone, and sinew if one tries to fight against a falling barrow load. I did, of course, the wrong thing. If I hadn't, I would have had a load of drying concrete sitting on top of the soil. At the time one doesn't think or notice one's pains, and I shoved a thigh against the side of the barrow and heaved till most of the mixture poured in the direction of the hole. I was able to use a trowel to shove the rest to its proper destination. Part of the trouble was caused by working late, in a hurry, into the near darkness. Only the next day, entering the shower, did I notice the large and vivid bruising on my inner thigh (which took a few weeks to clear).

The lessons so far: measure carefully, clear the surface of the area one is working in, let barrows fall, stop work before it gets too late to see clearly. One evening, finishing off the last hole, I kept going till I could no longer see the bubble in the carpenter's level. I unplugged the pond and hooked up a light onto a branch of the cedar, and did, satisfyingly, finish concreting the last post in place.

The next day I went out in the daylight to assess the work of the previous evenings. I measured across from corner to corner and was puzzled—the corners didn't . . . I stopped . . . what could be the problem? Why didn't I get the same measurement from corner to corner? Warily, I took the long set-square, and laid it next to the small straight 1" × 2" strips I had placed running along the lines of posts. I couldn't believe it. They were out of square. By a significant amount. How had I gone so wrong? I stood back and looked. The fences! They were not square! What a fool! I had built my posts in line with fences that were not themselves square. What could I do? The concrete had dried and was becoming immovable as I looked at it. Could I dig the posts out?

I stood looking at the two sides of what was to be the tea-house, and felt an awful sense of stupidity, helplessness, despair. I was near tears, of frustration and shame.

My wife had been out during the day, and came in just after I had cleaned and put away my tools. I told her about my gross mistake in measuring. She said, to my considerable comfort, that human beings do these kinds of things, and if the teahouse is to sit at a somewhat unsquare attitude to the world, well, so did we. It was indeed a comfort; my off-square teahouse was a product of the twisted nature of human beings, who never sit foursquare to the world. And within a while, I was almost recovered, almost laughing at my stupidity, and almost cheerfully accepting that this stupidity is a part of me and is what I have to work with, so I must accept its results and fare forward.

That night, feeling still a bit despondent after the day's major failure, I decided to watch TV rather than do something more constructive. Fate's rather sick sense of humor decided to put on for me a program on the Leaning Tower of Pisa, and the errors of its construction and the endless problems of trying to fix them. And, of course—and I tell you this in confidence— it was my own fence that created the problem, zigzagging as it does along the property line at the back of the garden.

Soon I should be putting in the long joists and the floor that would rest on them, and once that was done it would be very awkward doing anything to the earth beneath the teahouse. So this was the time to level the ground, adding a few more barrowloads to the rising piles behind the shrubs. Then I laid landscape fabric over every exposed inch of soil.

Laying down the landscape fabric, in the vain hope of discouraging weeds.

I had intended to dump more of the gravel I had put on the area along the fence, but made another mistake. I forgot to tell the stone merchant that I wanted compactible gravel, and said yes to pea-gravel, of the kind I had put on the top of the bog. It was dumped in the drive and I began barrowing it back and spreading it inches deep on top of the black fabric.

The posts surrounded by pea-gravel; the camera angle attempts to hide the posts' irregularities.

Only a week or so later did I realize that this gravel was not going to compact down and allow me to spread stones on top of it. I feared that I had just built the neighborhood's finest and most luxurious kitty-litter site, for the ecstatic indulgence of all the local cats, and my endless scooping distress. Not, I should hastily assure you, that I have anything against cats. They have been, after all, one of our most effective allies in the mammal world. All our domestic cats seem to have descended from the Libyan wildcats domesticated by the ancient Egyptians. In Egypt the cat was called, delightfully, *miu*. And the

Egyptians worshipped cats with good reason. It has been calculated that one mouse in a year can eat or destroy about 34 pounds of human food, and an adult rat can destroy as much as 1,000 pounds. An active cat can typically kill 500 rats in a year, and so prevent the destruction of 250 tons of food supplies. In Greco-Roman times, the cat was associated with the goddess Isis. The cult of Isis survived and thrived well into Christian times in Europe. (Isis played the sistrum, which was the likely source of a confused translation to "the cat and the fiddle.") The Christians of the Middle Ages tended to demonize competing religions and cast adherents of Isis as witches and devil worshippers. The association of Isis with cats thus led to cats being seen as familiars of witches. This demonizing was particularly actively attached to black cats, due to the nighttime rituals in the goddess's temples. Bits of superstition about black cats still survive. In the Middle Ages, however, at particular times cats, as associates of the devil, were slaughtered by the thousand. One result was that rats thrived, freed from the attentions of their most effective feline controllers, and one result of that was increasing outbreaks of plague. Between 1346 and 1351 the bubonic plague, carried by rats to humans, wiped out more than 20,000,000 people in Europe.

So I am not disrespectful of cats; I just don't relish their using the gravel underneath my teahouse for their relief. But before worrying about what to do about the cats, I would have to rescue this further mistake of laying down the wrong kind of gravel by making it into a design feature. In this case an opportunity presented itself almost immediately.

There is a short, steep decline from the neighbor's fence on the north to the level at which the teahouse is to be built. The pea-gravel just rolled down the incline, exposing the black landscape fabric in the three feet between the fence and the rear wall of the teahouse. The other anomaly still to be dealt with was the mound of stones dug out while making the fence

Here's what the small wall looks like at the back. I tossed pea-gravel in among the stones to hide any sign of the underlying landscape fabric.

and the pond. I had been throwing them ahead of me from job to job, most recently tossing them back against the neighbor's fence out of the way of the teahouse area. The solution to two problems in one go is especially satisfying. I used the stones to build a small supporting wall along the back of the teahouse area, and round to the front where it would prevent the pea-gravel from dribbling onto the lawn.

Building the subfloor

I was going to bolt a series of joists onto the posts, one joist on each side of each post. I had four rows of posts, so would need eight long joists running north–south, and another three or four to go along the back and to go east–west between the joists. The joists would extend three feet beyond the edge of the teahouse to support a balcony, from which one could look down at the fish and the pond. The balcony would stick out maybe a foot over the nearest edge of the pond.

The lumberyard delivered the wood and sheets of plywood to form the floor. This was going to be tricky, as the joists that stuck over the edge of the pond would also be the supports for the balcony fence that I would build to stop children, and me, from falling into the pond. But I could hardly do the drilling to fix those supports to the joists later while leaning out over the pond, if only because any drilling would have wood shavings falling onto the fish, who would probably try to eat it, thinking it was their flakes of food. I had bought that treated wood, impregnated with preservatives, which is no doubt toxic to fish.

Mind you, my first concern was that it would be toxic to me. Even though I set up the workbench in the garden, I thought I should wear a mask while cutting, as well as the usual protective glasses. I measured each piece of 2" × 8" joist, intending to shape them with a subdued upward slice at the end that would hang over the pond, to give them a somewhat Japanese style. I laid the first twelve-foot joist between the workbench and the back of a garden chair, and prepared to cut. First I fitted the mask over my nose and mouth, then the glasses, plugged in the circular saw, and approached the wood warily. I had also laid an old shower curtain where the sawdust would fall, as I didn't want it to damage the lawn, or get into the food chain by finding its way to the compost heap.

Breathing, which I felt was a good habit to keep up even when wearing a mask, glasses, and gloves, meant that my breath came out of my mouth, slid up the mask and under the glasses, fogging them up. I couldn't see the pencil line on the wood. After a few more breaths, I could hardly see anything. I pushed the glasses up onto my head. It looked as though I could have a choice of mask or glasses but not both. I elected to use the mask and see well, being careful to stand above the saw so that no splinters would be able to come up toward my face.

Within an hour or so, I had dispensed with the mask and

gone back to the glasses. It was now mid-October, and dusk was coming too early. I gave up and began early in the afternoon of the next day. After cutting all the timber, I thought I'd stain everything first. It was a lovely fall day, sunshine all day, and temperatures approaching 20° Celsius (68° Fahrenheit). I was going to paint all the supports in the same solid charcoal stain I had used on the fence. I had a new can and began shaking it around. But then I recalled the requirement that it remain dry for at least twenty-four hours, and I had just heard the weather forecast promising drenching rains for overnight and the next day—rains that didn't come.

In light of the weather forecast, I decided to build now and stain later. My main problem was what to do about the support posts for the balcony fence. The solution had come to me a few days earlier in my favorite planning place, bed. I was away on a trip near Toronto and, lying in the dark of some motel, I had suddenly seen a solution.

I began laying pairs of the heavy eleven-foot joists together, with bits of 4" × 4" between them. Then I sliced off corners of the 4" × 4"s that were to be the supports for the balcony fence to fit the Japanese-style slices I had made at the ends of the joists. The trick now was to fit the 4" × 4" posts at right angles to the ends of the joists and bolt them in place.

But after I managed to bolt my first pair of joists to a 4" × 4" at the pond end, I had the problem of how to fasten the whole unwieldy apparatus to the posts. I measured down seven and a half inches from the lowest post, nailed one of the 1" × 2" strips to it at that point, then, making sure the strip was exactly level, nailed it to the other posts. I then nailed another strip parallel to and level with that first one on the other side of the post. Then it was a matter of adding such strips to all the other sets of posts. Such cunning. I was very pleased with myself when I heaved the first set of joists over the posts and rested them on the 1" × 2" strips. I slid them

The support joists with the balcony rails.

carefully outward, making sure they were exactly even with the end of the rear post. The balcony supports were sticking up over the edge of the pond. Then I quickly screwed each joist onto the posts.

Having got them all up and in place, I then had the fun of drilling holes for the carriage bolts. But that wasn't so easy. I needed to buy a screw bit that would go through one 2" × 8" joist, then through the central 4" × 4", then through the other 2" × 8". In the hardware store I consulted the guy who had been giving me incredulous advice throughout this project— he seemed not to believe that I was really doing any of this. I mentioned my need to drill through the considerable distance, and so my need for a long drill bit.

"Why not measure carefully and go in one side with a regular bit then drill in from the other side to meet the hole."

"Because I would never get them exactly to meet, or perhaps meet at all."

He looked at me with his usual skeptical eye and agreed that I needed a longer bit. I bought a murderous-looking hard-metaled sharp-horned brute that would go through steel. But it was a wonder to work with. The joists were held in place by the screws, which would be wholly inadequate to support the weight of the teahouse, so I began driving the drill bit on its journey through the three pieces of wood.

It went in a quarter inch and slowed. I eased it out and tossed aside the wood shavings, then in another quarter inch, and out, and in, and in no time I was through, tapping a carriage bolt through the hole and fastening it at the other side. There are few things as satisfactory as a good tool doing its job. The joists were fixed in place, and now I could slice the tops off the posts where they stuck above the level of the joists.

With a delicious sense of impending triumph, I entered the tool rental shop. I was sure I had him this time. I needed to cut the tops off the 4" × 4"s that stuck up above the joists, to create a level base for the floor of the teahouse, and a small chain saw was ideal for the job. Having described what I needed to do, I asked for a chain saw, and he even came across the shop floor to join me as I examined the various models he had available. He described the pros and cons of the various chain saws on the wide shelf, and then added:

"Of course, what you really need for that job is a reciprocating saw."

Damn.

He described its advantages, and I relented yet again. I'm not sure he was right. It turned out to be a tough beast, and cost me a lot of trouble working sideways across the edge of the joists. He hadn't calculated the distance from the edge of

Drilling through joists and post, preparing for the carriage bolts.

the 2" × 8" added to the 4" × 4", and sold me a blade that was too short. Once I had begun and realized the problem, I was faced with the choice of unfastening the blade, unplugging, changing out of my muck-caked jeans, and returning to the shop for a longer blade, or keeping going and cutting halfway through on one side of each post and then again on the other. I chose the latter and finished the job with my arms weak as jellyfish from the brutal juddering of the powerful saw. I had expected it to work like a circular saw. But my forearms were numb after the first post, and ready to drop off at the elbows after the last.

Looking at the construction at this point, I suspect that someone ignorant of such things might assume I knew what I was doing. It was a curious sensation, looking at this construction through the eyes of a visitor. Do you suppose the builders of the pyramids or Stonehenge stood back as visitors admired their work, bemusedly reflecting on the concatenation of errors and guesses and compromises that nevertheless stood there confidently, set to sail forward forever on the ocean of time? No? You're probably right; they really did know what they were doing.

Lying awake during a trip to Ireland soon after cutting the posts level with the joists, jet-lagged, with water running all night long, inches from my head in the next room, I fretted that it was raining nonstop on the exposed freshly cut and unprotected stumps of the posts. Would water seep into the fibers and lead to their rotting, or could I still protect them by soaking in some preservative? Not the best topic for a wakeful night.

The insulated floor
The samurai who had slammed the black pine into place fiercely instructed me to water it heavily every day it didn't rain. I had set off to Ireland, asking my wife to please give it a soak on dry days. When I got back, she told me there hadn't been a dry day. Nor was there one for the following month. The newspapers began running stories about how there had been a wetter December in 1972, and we were still a few inches shy of the 1898 deluges. While this meteorological record saved me from having to water the pine, it also meant I was unable to get out and work. The contract for this book suggested I finish by May, which meant I needed to get the teahouse finished earlier, unless I wanted to move from description to imaginative fiction. Sitting watching the rain pummel the site each day, day after day, began to introduce some anxiety into what was supposed to be a casual hobby. On the shortest day of the year, suddenly, the skies cleared and we had one day of clear blue sky.

Lack of planning does lead one to interesting and unique situations. Alas, I realized that sometimes they are unique because no sane person would ever get him- or herself into them, which is no doubt why I can't find hints in any of my books for how to go about what seems the necessary next step. Because I wanted to insulate the floor, so that I could use the teahouse/study during the winter, I needed to nail a base to the bottom of the joists. On this base I would lay the insulation, staple some plastic over it, to make it proof against insects creeping up, and then on top of that put the thick plywood floor. Easy. Well, to do so I had to lie on my back on the peagravel, swinging a hammer close to my nose in the confined space, and nail sheets of thin plywood up against the bottom of the joists.

I thought it might be difficult, but my imagination couldn't prepare me for the reality. The quarter-inch plywood came in 2' × 8' strips. First I had to cut them so that they would slot neatly around the supporting posts. Then I pushed the strip over the gravel and under the joists, slotting the cut holes around the supports. What to do next? I stood with an old piece of carpet, designed to protect me from the damp gravel, wondering how I was to get it under the plywood, then get me on top of the carpet and under the plywood—in the foot and a couple of inches of space between the bottom of the joists and the gravel. As with everything, just begin.

Sitting on the strip of carpet at the rear of the teahouse and facing the pond, I slid my feet under the plywood. Then I pushed forward, knees getting under the plywood, then lying back and shuffling myself, pushing with elbows, till I had the plywood resting on my nose, knees and feet pushing it up against the joists further down. With impressive contortions— a tribute to my yoga instructor—I reached over my shoulder with one hand to grab the bag of nails and hammer, and with the other pushed the plywood firmly against the joists by my head. Holding the plywood firm with my forearm, I picked out a nail, held it in place, and drove the hammer head toward it at the only angle possible to me. The hammer struck it sideways, shooting it off somewhere onto the equally gray gravel. I tried another and hit my thumb. I edged to my left to get a better swing and, having so little space, held the hammer sideways to allow an extra inch or so. The third nail ended up stuck in my sweater somewhere. The fourth actually stuck into the wood. A few more hits and it was in place, followed by a further five or six nails along the rear edge. They went in with only minor damage to my fingers and thumb, and the spraying of maybe another half dozen nails around the gravel.

I then had to move downward toward the pond, pushing the plywood up with feet and knees as I went. There was nothing much to hold on to, and I was also trying to drag the piece of carpet along under me. Heels and elbows and a kind of horizontal waddle got me a few inches farther, and I began hammering again. Frequently I missed the joists above and would have to pull out the nail and try again. I worked out a way of squirming forward, helped by the occasional pull against a post, using muscles in my lower stomach that I think had long ago accepted a retirement package from the body's management. It took an hour of hammering in the confined space, each blow resounding close to an ear, but in the end the first piece of plywood was in place, ready to accept the slight burden of insulation.

With some relief I stood up, straightened, then measured and cut the second piece of plywood. I climbed under from the rear again, remembering pictures in childhood books of coal miners working a seam that was running out. My hammering was becoming a little more efficient, but efficiencies in technique were countered by aching muscles, particularly in the arm tying to swing the constrained hammer. I switched hands for a while, ensuring that I crunched fingers and thumb on the other hand as well. Slowly I squirmed toward the pond, the resounding hammering incessant, the sweat building despite the coldness of the day.

I finished that strip, emerged into the vertical world to cut the third piece of plywood, and crawled back into my confined hell. All the hammering was at odd angles, and it was hard to trace the line of the joists from one end to another. Also I was increasingly fogging up and was not going to give up the protective glasses as ill-hit nails might shoot in any direction. In the middle of this section, aching so that I could hardly lift the hammer, I passed it to the other hand. Then, just for some relief from the strained position, I began to turn, as one might in bed after lying too long on one's back. One shoulder stuck against the plywood and the other ground down into the gravel. I had nothing to lever against, was dog-tired, and thought I might just have to stay wedged like this till my wife came home to pull me out. I should have brought a cell phone in with me to call for help.

(When I later went into the house, I found that my wife had phoned and left a message. Not finding me in, she said how pleased she was that I was out working in the garden on this lovely, sunny day and congratulated me from her comfortable office.)

The good news under the plywood was that the pea-gravel was proving inhospitable to cats. Far from becoming kitty-litter central, I had not seen a cat on it and neither saw nor smelled any evidence of their relieving visits. Perhaps something about its shifting and clicky surface bothered them. Long may it do so!

Realizing that my wife might come home but never think of looking for me under the plywood, I eventually scraped and grunted myself free, and continued the slow drive down to the pond end, hammering and squirming. The third sheet had taken me longer than I had anticipated, and I was late for lunch. I pulled myself out, stood up, and felt nauseous, dizzy, and disoriented. I had been three hours on my back, using retired muscles, and wondering what on earth I was doing. I found myself constantly repeating, with varied purple words, the sentence that was becoming my mantra on this job: "I don't know what the x I'm doing!" This was, I later decided, not just a comment about the practical task at hand—I didn't know how to hammer properly, or to fit the plywood, or to consistently hit the joists—but about the whole enterprise. None of the jobs I had done, from the beginning, was really done properly. And such moments, confined under the plywood, pressed into damp and cold gravel, do tend to stimulate reflection on the whimsy with which I started the whole project. But there was no way out now except by finishing it.

Lunch, followed by tea and cookies over the paper, revived my spirits a bit, and I found myself later looking down at another sheet of plywood, with the old piece of carpet beneath it. I stood looking for a while, physically reluctant to squeeze my body between the two. An act of will dragged me to a sitting position, then shoved my feet under the plywood, then impelled the lower-stomach squirm till the plywood rested on my nose while I grabbed backward for the nails and hammer.

The black underworld where I nailed plywood up to the joists, and where I spent many cheerful hours reciting my mantra.

The hardest action was moving forward once I was about halfway down toward the pond. There was nothing to lever myself against. I could squirm to and fro, but, unless I wanted to rest my head in the damp gravel, I needed at the same time to drag the carpet with me. The trouble was that I was lying on the carpet and couldn't raise myself from it without banging my head against the plywood. By bending one arm in ways I don't think the joints were designed for, and giving tiny pushes against the other elbow and minileaps from lower stomach, then pulling and sliding at the same time, I could manage to progress an inch or two, keeping the carpet more or less under my head. The further trouble was that each slide brought more bits of gravel onto the carpet, so that by the time I reached the pond end, it wasn't clear that I was any better off with my head in the gravel on the carpet than I would have been without the carpet altogether.

As I put each piece of plywood above me, I added to the problem the afternoon was bringing on this shortest day of the year. As I shrugged and squirmed down the last strip, I could hardly see what I was doing. I only became conscious of the combined effects of the setting sun, the layer of plywood above me, the misting and dust-bespattered protective glasses, when I realized I was hitting my fingers more often than the nails and could hardly see the nails. For the last few on the final sheet, I had to take off the glasses even to be able to work out the rough area I was aiming at. But gradually the nails found their way through the plywood into the joists and the final sheet was ready, and I lay back too exhausted to feel satisfied. No doubt I could get used to this, but I think I'd rather not.

The following morning I couldn't raise myself from bed. The stomach muscles that normally do the job were tied up in some way with the newfound muscles I had used in the squirm and were refusing further work without exacting a massive price in pain. I was able to roll over and off the bed, and was fine once I stood up. Getting into the shower, I noticed a string of bruises down the inside of my left arm, but couldn't think what action had been responsible. Odd requiring one's aging body to do work the younger mind would never have envisioned. But, apart from a few patches, the plywood was in place, and now I could move on to the relatively simple tasks of putting in the insulation, hammering down the thick plywood floor, framing and roofing and living happily ever after. Boxing Day was the next chance to do more work. There were a few gaps in the base plywood that needed filling in. The circular saw slices thin plywood like paper, and in a few minutes I had cut pieces for each of the gaps. But then I had to climb under again and felt quick though muted nausea as I dragged myself beneath the floor across the gravel. By now I was quite practiced with hammer and nails in a confined space and had all the holes blocked within an hour. I also discovered how I had bruised the underside of my left arm—getting leverage against the rear joist as I heaved myself out again.

It was a relief to work vertically, and slotting the pink insulation on top of the thin plywood went easily.

I stapled a film of plastic over the whole surface area, laid the thick sheets of plywood that were to be the floor on top of the plastic, and then was called to go to lunch with grandchildren Joshua and Jordan. Jordan had been born about the time Joshua was looking into the hole that had housed Moby Rock for a little while. I suppose this garden project is just a redirecting of those terrible energies we expend on bringing up children. Ours had now all left home, and what's a dad to do then?

Framing

I bought a bunch of 2" × 4"s, read a bunch of books, and started the framing for the teahouse. The books usually assume you know the most basic things that you can't really start without knowing, but which I didn't know. Like what size

The insulated floor.

nails one should use. As usual, the first three people I asked in hardware stores each gave different answers. But the carpenters next door concurred, confidently, with the growing consensus around the three-inch common bright nail.

Framing gives the most to show for the least effort. Within a couple of hours I had the rear wall ready and standing. I should try to find out who first thought of making walls mostly of space. The intuitive way of going about building a wall was to lay down cut stones one on top of the other, or cut logs to fit one on top of the other, or place planks one against another. But this idea of making a relatively slender frame and then attaching the weatherproofing and insulation to it is really clever. This system of lightweight wood framing seems to have originated in Chicago around 1830. For one thing, it democratized building. Previously, using the heavy post and beam system, a team of men was required to raise a wall, but now even such as I could nail the frame of the wall together on the floor and lift the completed frame into place. And refined carpentry skills weren't required. Whereas in the past, the wall-builder needed to be able to make good mortise-and-tenon joints, all we need to do now is batter the relatively slender wood together with three-inch bright nails.

Framing was halted after the first successful day by further rain, and by children being home for Christmas and the whole family taking off to an island cabin we had rented for the turn of the millennium. And then was slowed by more rain. I began the second side of the teahouse frame on the first rain-free day, only to realize that I couldn't do much until I knew exactly what dimensions I should leave for the window. Shopping for doors and windows, I discovered, is not like getting a new pair of socks.

The first place I stopped at I was greeted by a large Asian man who sat behind a laptop computer in the rear of a display shop full of attractively finished windows and doors. I located his voice by peering at angles through about four different windows. I told him I wanted a door, with a round window, sand-blasted to echo the opaqueness of shoji-paper windows, a large nonopening 5' × 4' window at the front, behind which I would build a desk, two 4' × 3' windows for the west and east walls, and two 1' × 4' nonopening windows for the sides of the alcove, in case I decided I could fit one in.

Beginning the framing. The chair in the picture is my sawhorse; pieces of wood rest on the workbench and stretch out to the back of the chair.

He typed each item into his computer, but seemed to be taking an enormous amount of time. After a considerable while, I realized he was drawing each window to scale using his mouse. I said I was just hoping to get some general sense of the kinds of windows he could suggest, and their cost.

"This way will make it all faster down the road," he assured me, smiling at the screen. I'm not sure that his eyes left the computer screen all the time I was there. Also, I wasn't sure what "down the road" meant. I sat twiddling my thumbs as he worked away on the computer. I couldn't imagine what he was doing. After a while, I said I had to leave, as my wife wanted the car for the afternoon—all true.

"Just a moment now, just a moment." He spoke with real urgency. "I'm nearly there. Just the finishing touches."

Clearly, I was grossly trying to rush an artist. He hit a key hard, raised the hand high in the air on the rebound, and smiled seraphically at his creation.

"It's printing now," he said.

Across the showroom, a printer did indeed begin to whir, and I followed him toward it, relieved that he could walk and was not physically attached to the computer. He proudly handed me three pages of details, with, indeed, little pictures of each item in each section. Around the diagrams was a mass of information, mostly following abbreviations which meant nothing to me (DBL CLR NAC), though I could guess, and occasionally using whole words, which I couldn't understand (e.g., "brickmould"), though I later found out what they meant. Just to make it easier, all the dimensions were given in millimeters. The only translation into feet and inches was for cubic feet. Thus the ¼" = 1' scale picture of the 5' × 4' window was to be 7.373702 cubic feet. (I had first imagined a very large window, but then realized I might have difficulty also fitting a door on the same wall if I didn't constrain my imagination, so reduced it to 4' × 4'.)

As a product of massive investment in time on the computer this was all somewhat mystifying. But each item did have a price attached, down to the penny. The next day, when I could have the car again, I visited a couple of other places, and was given quick and workmanlike quotes. Sitting at home at my desk with the three sets of quotes in front of me, I felt about as bewildered as when I began. The prices quoted varied by hundreds of dollars. What was the ignorant consumer to make of this? The computer man wanted $1,342.61 for the door, whereas the man I liked most and who was enthusiastic about the project when I told him what I was doing quoted $754. Would the cheaper one fall to pieces in a few weeks? The middle quote was for $980. The computer man wanted $410.38 for each of the 1' × 4' windows, whereas the pleasant guy wanted $159.

I phoned each of them and explained my quandary. Perhaps the computer calculated for gold hardware? When I talked to the middle quoter, he expressed surprise that his competitor a few blocks away was quoting so much less. I asked what there was about his door and windows that might make them so much more expensive ($525 for the 4' × 3' windows as against the $381 quoted by my good friend up the road). There was a moment of panic and an admission that the competitor "made a good product too." He phoned back later to offer revised figures, but by then I had contacted the friendlier Rob, and we were to meet to get all the final details sorted out—which way the door was to open and so on. Rob was so keen on the project that I thought he might offer the door and windows for free. Oddly, he didn't.

Another afternoon of framing between the rainstorms, and I had two walls up. The hard part was pushing the walls up to a vertical position once I had nailed all the pieces together. I should have had help, but, as usual, no one was around. The first wall frame had gone up without too much trouble, though it was heavier than I had expected. That was the rear wall. I had nailed 2" × 4"s onto each side to brace the wall and prevent it from falling forward. The cedar tree was behind it and would prevent it falling that way. The next wall to go up was the one facing east, overlooking the bamboo and fence. I wasn't sure how to support it, as I could fit a 2" × 4" brace only on one side. I heaved it up, and felt a sudden panic as it swayed and threatened to keep going over. It would have smashed the fence and crushed the bamboo. I hung on to it desperately, pulling it back. I leaned down with one hand and grabbed another eight-foot-long 2" × 4" and slotted it against the window frame, hammering it in to make another brace. I added a couple more, then climbed up to the top to nail a temporary short brace across the two walls.

Sitting at my desk the next morning, I saw a huge backhoe

operating in the garden beyond my Japanese-style fence. It seems Shirley and Jerry, of the japonica quince and empty lot to the east, had finally sold the land, and the new owners were doing as Shirley had predicted, leveling the whole surface of the garden. At least that would be the end of the bindweed, I hoped. As the monster came closer to my fence, I went out to recommend they preserve the quince.

I couldn't see how much clearing they had done. When one of the workers looked up, I waved, and he came across to the fence. I shouted, over the roaring of the backhoe, that he might be interested to preserve the beautiful quince just behind the fence.

"Don't worry. It's all gone!" he shouted, waving cheerfully. So my attempt to liberate half the quince was sort of justified.

I did something a while ago to strain my elbows, perhaps connected with lugging around too heavy stones. Now I have exacerbated the problem by the heavy bouts of hammering and seem to have developed "tennis elbow," or "golfer's elbow," or perhaps both. Lifting a phone after a day of wielding the hammer is agony. Aching at those joints most noticeably, and at all the others too (as I wouldn't want your sympathy to be too localized), creates an odd dilemma. Normally when I strain something and am in pain, I go to the doctor or physiotherapist and learn that I must rest it and do the following set of impossible-to-remember exercises, twenty of each, three times, twice a day, or something. But I can't rest from this job, or the skeletal frame will sit there for weeks. Indeed, I learned the term golfer's elbow from a friend who claimed to have it and described symptoms just like mine. I didn't confess to having it also, as he had a brace on his arm and was using it as little as possible. I am having to try the alternative therapy of ignoring it and hoping it will go away, bored by neglect.

There is something in this approach of ignoring pain, I'm

sure. I read a study some years ago that recommended going off painkillers after an operation as quickly as possible. The pain was greater initially but went away much more quickly, the study claimed. I had been, at that time, having the second of identical knee operations. With the first surgery, I had followed the usual routine—powerful painkillers in the first days, gradually reduced over a few weeks till the pain was more or less gone. It took nearly a month of considerable discomfort. (The operation was fairly nasty and involved screws of carbon, molybdenum, and nickel in the shinbones—not three screws but the three elements in each screw!) After the second operation, I decided to give up painkillers as soon as I left hospital. The first two days were bad, but as the study predicted, by the third or fourth day, my brain had clearly decided pain was boring and gave up registering it.

What is fairly frustrating as I hammer away, bending the occasional nail and having to tug it out, is hearing the guys begin work on a new house over the fence. The pneumatic thump and hiss of their power nail guns make me and my aching elbows feel a bit envious. I'd buy one if I didn't fear nailing myself to a wall with it.

These winter days when it isn't raining, I carry out the workbench and a box of tools, and begin to measure and cut 2" × 4"s. There are moments of exasperation when I measure, carefully, I think, and make a pencil mark on the wood, then extend the mark into a neat line with a set square, then cut carefully with the circular saw, and find that the cut piece of wood is a quarter-inch short. How does it happen? But mostly, by being even more careful, I manage to cut the wood to the right size, lay it out on the floor, then nail it together. The framing goes quickly, and from a suitable distance (measured in miles) looks quite professional.

As I stand at the workbench, in the old black coat my father had bought just before he died, the mind relaxes, and odd thoughts drift through. This morning I read in the paper that the Galileo spacecraft has recently flown by Jupiter's moon Europa. Measurements of the moon's magnetic field apparently support the theory that the moon is made up of an icy crust, some miles below which there is a watery ocean. As I lean over the next 2" × 4" and coax the saw blade along the pencil line, I feel Europa somewhere out there, with its waters swirling. My other relaxing pastime on this magnificent coast of North America is kayaking, and for a moment I realize that as I am cutting here now, very particular waves at particular points on Europa are moving restlessly, as water pulled by celestial neighbors moves. So far from the sun, and under a thick surface of ice, the waters would be dark. A while ago, a little foolhardily, I was in a kayak at night on English Bay, gradually coming in toward the lighted high-rises of Vancouver's West End. I was far enough away for the city to be silent, with just the noise of the waves and paddle slicing the water. Somewhere on Europa, on its dark interior ocean—I imagine idly as the cut end of the 2" × 4" falls—one might kayak. Protective suiting and an oxygen pack might change the feel a tad from a spring evening in English Bay. Jupiter's enormous nearby heaving force keeps Europa's core warm, and who knows what waves that force piles up in that dark ocean. All very well, the mind says, but it's time to cut the headers for the windows, and less attention to Europa and more to the measuring tape might be in order.

Now I have done something rather shameful and a bit embarrassing, and I think I need the break to a new chapter to build up the courage to tell you about it.

eight

Inhabiting the teahouse/study

Now THIS EASY AND PLEAS-
ant pastime of knocking bits of wood together until the teahouse is completed has become a bit pressured, and you, I'm
sorry to say, aren't entirely blameless. My kind editor assures
me that you are, although unaware of the book at this point
of my writing, subconsciously clamoring to buy multiple
copies for Christmas. For this sensible outcome to enter the
world of the possible, she needs the manuscript finished in less
than two months. If the weather continues as it has been, this
seems hopeless. Also I do have a job that my employers incon-
siderately expect me to spend time at. As the writing can only
follow the building, and the building is hampered by weather
and other work, I conclude that, if I am to satisfy your entirely
understandable desire to buy the book, I need help.

Getting a carpenter
It has been a kind of exasperating fun hammering the tea-
house/study together. I have become increasingly confident
that the wood will all stand up if I attach it together with
enough sturdy metal bolts, nails, and screws. But I must
research and read so much about how to do it that even in

ideal weather conditions, completing everything will require more than the luck of the Irish. So with some regret I have asked Brendan, a carpenter, if he will give me a hand.

He looks over what I have done so far, and he may be lying through his teeth or hiding a smirk of pity, but he says it isn't too bad. I ask how long it might take him, with my help, to get the framing finished. I have been calculating about three more weeks.

"Oh, I think we can have the roof on in two days."

Suddenly it begins to look possible.

Brendan has turned up in the mornings for the past three days. He cuts and hammers, expertly, and the teahouse has exploded upward into the unsuspecting sky. I have been thinking of the teahouse construction in terms of Stonehenge or the pyramids, and it has been a little sobering, standing on my floor under the skeleton of Brendan's roof, to have him say, "This is a nice little project."

He brings his dog with him, a large black beast of indeterminate breed. But he is the friendliest animal and sits contentedly in Brendan's truck or sniffs around at the end of a long lead, delighted to be patted.

"I got him six years ago after someone ripped off my tools. My dad said that a dog in the cab would be the perfect deterrent, and he was right."

We chatted for a while about what we might do to give the roof a distinctive shape and overhang. I wanted a low-pitched roof with quite a wide overhang at the sides and extending forward to shelter the deck. After about ten minutes the dog started barking at the other end of the garden. Brendan said only, "The boss. Time to get back to work." And, indeed, as soon as Brendan started sawing and hammering, the dog was quiet.

As I see Brendan hopping around on the roof, I think getting help wasn't a bad idea at all.

I had imagined that I would be helping Brendan as he

Brendan framing the roof.

worked, but, watching his practiced ease, I realize that I would as likely slow him down as help. So I leave him to work on the teahouse while I try to fix up various so far unfinished features of the garden as a whole. Also I work at this text when I can.

The framed alcove.

One feature of the teahouse that I included in my vague plans, then rejected as too problematic, and included again, and rejected again, is a small alcove at the rear corner flanked by two tall thin windows. I had decided, reluctantly, that the cedar tree was too close, and that I wouldn't be able to make the alcove wide enough to put a seat between the windows. I mentioned the idea to Brendan, who smiled; within a few hours, he had the thing framed, the floor extended backward a couple of feet and supported with 2" × 8"s bolted onto the base posts. Adding the alcove, I have discovered, is a bit presumptuous. It seems that up to the end of the Edo period in Japan (1615–1868), building an alcove was a privilege available only to samurai and rich merchants. I don't qualify on either score, but there it is with the window spaces ready on either side.

Perhaps you are disappointed that someone else is so heavily involved in the project at this point. I feel somewhat ambivalent about it, as there is a sense of loss that the results will not be wholly of my own making, but also there is a sense of wonder and delight at Brendan's swift and competent work. At least I can sit in the finished teahouse/study confident that the roof won't come down on me.

Having betrayed the idea that I would build the whole garden myself—though I don't think this was ever more than a subconscious desire—I couldn't shake the feeling that I was repeating something, but I couldn't put my finger on what. Then I remembered that this whimsical enterprise of building the garden, and then writing about it as I went, echoed in a minor key Hilaire Belloc's buoyant and vivacious *The Path to Rome* (Harmondsworth: Penguin, 1958). I found my old copy of the book and the passage my own plight reminded me of.

On a whim one day, Belloc vowed to walk from the valley of the Moselle, where he was born, to Rome, doing thirty miles a day; his goal was to attend Mass in St. Peter's Basilica on the feast of St. Peter and St. Paul. As he walked, he described the people he met, the adventures he had, and his thoughts and feelings. Once into Italy, exhausted by heat, and unable to cover the distance toward Rome in time, he entered a church to pray and rest and decide what to do. There were two candles nearly burned out. As he watched their slow race to extinction, he decided that his choice of whether to keep on walking and risk illness or to take a train across the plain of Lombardy to Milan would be determined by which of the two candles remained alight longer:

> They were a long time going out, and they fell evenly. At last the right hand one shot up the long flame that precedes the death of candles: the contest took on interest, and even excitement, when, just as I thought the left hand certain of winning, it went out without guess or warning. . . . The right hand candle waved its flame still higher, as though in triumph, outlived its colleague just the moment to enjoy glory, and then in its turn went fluttering down the dark way from which they say there is no return.

Unlike Belloc, I can't claim that the gods insisted I get significant help with this last stage of the project, but I suspect my journey is also more likely to be completed as a result.

Choosing colors
To meet the editor's deadline, I decided to take my annual holiday early, so that I could be out working on the garden, or in, as now, writing about working on the garden. For a week or so the days had a regular pattern. Brendan arrived and set to work on the teahouse, we consulted on various design features or discussed what needed to be done next, and I set to work on completing the garden.

Now that the garden is done, we can work together on the teahouse. He has finished the framing, has the roof shingled and tarpaper around the whole. We chose a local cedar shingle that is sturdy, handsome, and likely to last twenty years. His method of putting on the tarpaper, which protects against

Darth Vader's teahouse.

moisture while allowing some ventilation for the wood, is simply to go around the whole structure, covering windows as well. As I sit here, peering through the marginal pond plants, to whom I am providing the hospitality of my study during winter, I look out on this black-clad structure. It seems like the kind of teahouse Darth Vader or Batman might have contemplated.

In the basement downstairs is the treated plywood that will form the outside wall. We will paint it inside the house, as it is presently too cold to paint outside. Brendan picked up the wood yesterday, and my job was to choose and pick up the paint. I had admired the effectiveness of the solid color stain I had used on the fence, and went back to the mega hardware store where I had bought it. I took along one of my Japanese gardening books, with a picture of a teahouse with just the ocher/mustard color I wanted.

There was no other customer at the paint area, so I easily got the attention of the three "paint associates." First the elderly

Chinese man looked at the picture and selected some of those tiny slips of card that indicate the endless range of colors they can mix. He went to get some more cards and another folder or two, till we had every shade between a greeny ocher and an orangy mustard that the human eye can distinguish, or at least my human eye. By this time the other two associates were leaning over, indicating which of the tiny blobs of color they considered most like that of the pictured teahouse.

A young woman manager was drifting by, looked over to see what the interest was, elbowed her way in, and began offering her opinion. I stood back and let them go at it for a few moments. All four had different preferences and were arguing, most pleasantly, among themselves. I think I could have gone away and no one would have noticed or cared.

It is a desperate business trying to decide on the color of the main part of a building based on a tiny half-inch square of color on a white chart. The sensible thing would be to buy tiny pots of the three or four best choices, take them home, test them on pieces of wood, let them dry, and then decide. But all that would add a couple of days to the project, and time is running out. We are now into February. I settled on a slightly dull mustard, thinking I could always repaint it later if it seemed too cheerful.

Brendan wants to get the windows in next, so we have to stain them on the outside and varnish the inside. They are to be delivered in a couple of hours, so here I am at the computer catching up on yesterday's paint buying. These minutes are due to be interrupted by the pinger announcing that the cookies are ready. On his first day, I asked Brendan if he would like a cup of tea, and took it out with a couple of cookies. He enjoyed these so much that a regular part of my day involves making tea and bringing out cookies. And this requires my making sure there are cookies to take out. I make them from one of those premixed batters, so it is no great culinary feat to slap blobs onto a cookie sheet and bake them. But it isn't one of the tasks I'd expected to be involved in while building the teahouse.

Now if you could see the windows and door piled in the basement, you would have to concede that my painting is not obviously worse than Brendan's. It's just that he does it at about six times the speed I do. I am a very careful painter—Sistine Chapel kind of pace—and after two days of putting three coats of solid color stain on what will be the outside of the windows, and four coats of varnish on the inside, I am ready to volunteer to climb under the teahouse and nail up some more plywood—even though Brendan did most of the work.

I had imagined moving at a slow pace through the spring and summer, gradually building and making leisurely decisions about each next step. But Brendan is asking for decisions on the color of this, how to shape that, where to put the other. Usually he has some excellent suggestions and saves me floundering around. He had brought samples of cedar for the soffits—the exposed area at the sides and front of the teahouse under the eaves. Did I want them stained? Solid color or semi-transparent? What color? Clear cedar or knotty (the latter being half the price of the former)? Somehow in the conversation, bamboo was mentioned. Brendan said we could indeed make the soffits of bamboo.

In some of the books I had seen pictures of the underside of overhangs covered in bamboo, but had assumed that bamboo would be too difficult to work, and that the right kind of bamboo would be unavailable. Then I remembered that the landscape supply center had plenty in various sizes. Brendan calculated what we would need, and I drove over and ordered it. They delivered the dozen twelve-foot poles within a couple of hours—one benefit of working at the raw and unfashionable end of February. Using Brendan's table saw, we cut the poles in two, though he later discovered it was easier and neater to splice them. Bamboo's fibers are precisely vertical, so one need only hammer an ax-head to cut the top and it slices into neat halves all the way down. It would now be a matter of drilling small holes through the halves and nailing them to the rafters, curved sides showing. They had the further advantage that I wouldn't have to worry about staining them, nor about what kind of system to fix up to allow ventilation into the roof. The bamboo slices laid side by side would allow perfect ventilation. A layer of mesh behind them would serve to keep out any marauding insects.

As I go out at the end of a day to see how the teahouse is coming along, there are occasional unplanned delights. Looking through the frame that will hold the garden-side window, I was greeted by heavy nodes of small pink blossoms from our old winter flowering jasmine nodding familiarly.

Brendan seems as enthusiastic as I ought to be about this project. He told me yesterday how he is the envy of his carpenter colleagues, because he gets these really interesting jobs. I hadn't thought of it like that and guess it must be more fun for a skilled woodworker to be able to improvise, make suggestions, and discover techniques for using bamboo than to zap in wall studs at sixteen-inch intervals for new houses.

One of the losses connected with Brendan's contribution to the project is in my interactions with suppliers. While I am hardly the chatty type, I have enjoyed discussing the project and getting advice from so many different people. I have one friend who manages during the filling of his car with gas to get on so well with the attendant that by the time the tank is full he knows the birth dates of each of the man's children and has an invitation to the eldest's wedding. This project has supplied an excuse to get beyond my usual reticence, even if I can't aspire to my friend's communicative league. But now, instead of chats with Rob about what kind of window-framing material I might need, the exchanges are more like this morning's phone call:

Bamboo soffits and winter-flowering jasmine.

"Hi, Kieran. Rob here. Brendan's in picking up some framing material. Shall I charge it to your Visa?"

"Sure."

"Thanks. Bye."

Yesterday I added a further coat of solid-color stain to the exterior wall panels, on the principles that it's easier to do it now and the more coats the better protection.

How does one apply stain to ten sheets of 4' × 8' plywood panels in the small entry area of a basement? I followed Brendan's procedure. One begins by laying the ten sheets one on top of the other on the floor, and clearing a nearby area of wall against which one can stand them. Then one unscrews the handle from a brush and screws it into the end of a paint-roller. With a large dollop of stain in a paint tray, one dips in the roller head and starts rolling the stain onto the top sheet of plywood. The rolling takes only a few minutes, and is the pleasant part of the job. When finished staining, one then has to lift the sheet of plywood onto a couple of pieces of 2" × 4" near the wall, slotting at the top another small piece of 2" × 4" to prevent the stain making a neat line across the wall. Then one sets about the second sheet on the floor, lifting it onto the 2" × 4"s by the wall when finished, and slotting another chunk of wood between sheet two and sheet one. And so on down the set of ten sheets. And there they stand, with a fan at the end encouraging them to dry.

I read that the average yearly production of plywood would allow one to lay a panel 12 feet wide from the end of our garden or from downtown Philadelphia to the moon. Or at least it would be allowed were it not for some inconvenient physical laws. Plywood is made from thin veneers of wood glued together, the grain of alternating layers at right angles to each other. The product of this ingenious arrangement is astonishing strength for its weight. While these thin slabs are crucial to so much modern building, it is hard to feel a lot of affection for plywood. There's something a bit geekish about it—clever, useful, and eager to help, but deficient in character. Mind you, it is not as bad as those composite woods. You knock on them and a dead sound greets your alarmed knuckles.

In the end I decided to stain the trim the same green as the fence. The problem with all the pieces of trim is what to do with them in an already overfull basement once they are covered in wet green stain. On the first day, after finishing work on the windows, I had time only to begin and decided to do all the smaller pieces. I was quite proud of my ingenuity. Taking a couple of two-foot pieces of spare 2" × 4"s, I tapped in nails of varying sizes sloping backward. Once I had stained a piece of trim, I laid it against the rear nails across the 2" × 4"s. Each of the other pieces of stained trim was leaned against a further couple of nails. I had to go to work the following day, despite holidays, and Brendan came to stain and

Beginning to look as though we might finish it in time.

varnish what remained. He tacked nails to the vertical beams in the basement and had the longer pieces of trim stained and neatly stacked one above the other when I came home.

When sadistic medieval committees sat down to decide on what precisely a gallon should be, they calculated very carefully just how much paint would be needed on the average job centuries hence, ensuring that the gallon can would contain just a tiny bit too little for whatever job one had on hand. Another of Murphy's laws.

We are now ready to put in the windows and to nail on the outside layer of plywood and the trim. Each piece has multiple layers of stain or varnish, and my wife would like to be able to navigate through the basement without tripping over paint cans. But we have had a couple of days of heavy rain, and Brendan has booked into an indoor job for the next two days, in the hope that we'll get better weather later in the week.

Another problem this sudden speed of construction has created is financial. I had been expecting to work gradually at the teahouse and garden till the summer, buying wood, stones, dry wall, and tatami mats as I could afford them. But now I have to shell out daily, pouring sackfuls of loot into the eager hands of hardware store investors, window manufacturers, lumberyard owners, and on and on. I have had to spend as much time at the bank as in lumberyards of late, arranging lines of credit to finish this extravaganza.

Planning the interior

Brendan has worked so fast completing the exterior, using his power nail-driver to fix the stained panels to the sides, putting in the windows, adding trim all around, that I find myself having to study books that will help me decide what to do with the interior. The best I have found is Koji Yagi's *A Japanese Touch for Your Home* (Tokyo: Kodashna International, 1982).

The easy part, I thought, was the floor. Tatami mats would cover the base of the teahouse. They are made from a rice straw core, covered with a woven soft reed skin, and finished off around the edges with a cloth border. They are quite heavy, but are delightful to the touch, excellent insulators, and very sturdy. I had long ago cut an ad from a local magazine for Japanese products and now decided I needed to visit the showroom and see how much further enough tatami mats to cover the floor would set back my bank imbalance. The ad said that one needed to phone to make an appointment.

While Brendan finished putting on siding and trim, and fitting the bamboo soffits under the eaves, I drove out to my appointment with Mr. Lee. His office is in one of those industrial streets, with low warehouselike buildings, that seem like some Soviet bureaucrat's notion of efficient planning. A dull street, broken by the bridge of the SkyTrain in the distance. Set back from the road were the two-story bunkers, monotone, grim, windows at the front fashionably tinted in dark colors with shutters blocking any sense of humans inside. They were separated from the road by a broad stretch of colorless stones, with clumps of weeds poking through; what appeared to be the dead stumps of trees chain-sawed down to knee level added to the sense of desolation. Inside, the building had bare cinderblock walls and narrow stairs about ten feet ahead, cheaply carpeted. I was about to head up them, but noticed immediately to my right a door, the same dun color as the inside wall of the building. There was a small card pinned to it announcing Japanese products.

I pressed the bell, and Mr. Lee invited me in with a friendly handshake. I had been prepared to bow, though Mr. Lee was clearly Chinese, not Japanese. A year earlier, when visiting Mike and Tanya in Nagoya, I had been waiting in the airport when a group of about four or five Japanese businessmen arrived to greet a similar-sized group of visiting American businessmen. Each had obviously been studying the customs of the other; the Americans all bowed from the waist as the Japanese held out their hands to be shaken.

From the brutal industrial exterior, I walked into a room of beautiful and delicate Japanese constructions. There was a raised platform of tatami mats, shoji lamps and screens, antique wall hangings, minimally patterned sliding-door covers with white-feathered cranes among pines and bamboo overlying mountain scenes, with perfectly proportioned and fitted fir trim around the walls. One doesn't have to experience many such contrasts, or spend much time in Japan, to recognize why they consider us barbarians.

The tatami mats are available only in 3' × 6' sizes, a shade over two inches deep. We spent some time trying to work out how best to cover my irregular floor most economically, as they also charge $60 for each cut that has to be made. Mr. Lee explained seriously that cutting the mats is difficult to do well and has to be done by hand, and then a new cloth band needs to be sewn on. It became clear that my awkwardly sized teahouse floor would cost a fortune to cover in tatami.

I considered the Japanese sandals, and thought I might take four pairs, so that guests might slip them on at the door of the teahouse, leaving their shoes outside. And a couple of Japanese lamps for the wall. But they would be useless for reading, as the shoji paper restricted them to 25 watts. Such a room should have subdued lighting, to encourage quiet in one's soul. As I looked around, there were so many possibilities that Mr. Lee suggested that I should simply make notes, and come back when I was sure what I wanted. Driving away, I feared that the tatami mats were going to be much more expensive than I had expected, and that perhaps I should consider some other kind of flooring. But I realized that if I simply took three mats and laid them side by side, it would leave me with just about a foot spare all around. I could lay fir or some other wood between the mats and the wall.

Mr. Lee had recommended that I visit one of his competitors to see further options. I had mentioned that some pictures suggested that I might have bamboo on the ceiling of the teahouse, or planks of fir or cedar, with strips of bamboo across them. The best source for bamboo in the city, he said, is Elaine's. He phoned to make sure she was open, and sent me off with another gracious handshake.

I described to Elaine what I was trying to build, and said that I was considering bamboo for the interior ceiling of the structure, and wondered what kinds of bamboo she had. At the front of the shop she showed me thin bright yellow reed strips, woven into six-foot-by-fifteen-foot mats, then a slightly thicker pole fence bamboo. Either, she said, could be simply stapled onto the rafters. I looked around at the further possibilities. I had come in search of a single kind of bamboo, and would have been happy with that single choice, but faced with so many possibilities I was feverishly trying to locate the best, and think of what other surfaces I might cover in bamboo.

"So many possibilities!" I said.

She laughed and invited me to come to the rear of the shop. We passed an elderly Chinese man making roll-blinds from bamboo slices at a large workbench, and wandered through mountains of burlap bags full of bamboo poles from a quarter inch to five inches, and up to fifteen feet long, in endless shades of yellows, browns, greens. She seemed amused as I examined them, wondering at their variety and beauty, and said they could cut them in half for mounting on the ceiling, if I wished to do that. Then we wandered through a delicate forest of hanging roll-blinds, brown, tortoise-shell, white and off-white, multipatterned, till I couldn't calculate the possibilities of what I might be able to use. Like Mr. Lee, she laughed and invited me to make notes, visit their site on the Internet, and then come back when I had decided.

So that's what I did. I measured up all the walls and ceiling and floor spaces to be covered, then came home, drew some diagrams of each surface, and began planning what to put where.

For the wiring of the teahouse/study, I phoned an electrician who has done work for us in the past, with whom we get on well, what the Italians call my electrician *di fiducia*—my trusted electrician, though in Italy the term is used almost universally about any tradesperson. They are all *di fiducia,* suggesting that one has particular access to the very best. I asked if he could do the job soon.

"Tomorrow."

"I'll be away tomorrow."

"Leave the keys in the usual place. Stick a card where you want things, lights, plugs, etcetera."

I came back that evening, and there was a new conduit tube fixed onto the fence to the back of the garden, and all the wiring was in place. I still haven't seen the electrician. But he will be back when the dry wall is up to finish off.

While I take a break in the writing for more cookie making, Brendan is out fixing the final spliced bamboo poles under the eaves. They look great; a rich brown, with hints of green and yellow that shine dully with reflected light. These bamboo canes were innocently growing in China not long ago and now find themselves mounted on the underside of a hybrid teahouse/study in Canada. We'll never untangle this world now.

There is something bizarre about sitting here at the computer, looking out at Brendan cutting and tapping on the last of the trim. I find myself wondering how he is going to get up to the top peak under the roof to put in the final pieces of the wall panel and am fascinated by the ingenuity and speed with which he nails up 2" × 4"s from the front and rear sides of the teahouse to the balcony rails, then stretches a long 2" × 8" from front to back, and, lo, he has a small scaffold neatly in place. While he is doing this, I keep pausing and looking out. How does one compare, as kinds of work, a couple of paragraphs with a neat scaffold, and a few further sentences with measuring and cutting the final panel, climbing onto the scaffold and nailing it into place? The invention of writing has confused so much for us.

The commonest criterion for comparing kinds of work these days is money, of course. Based on how long I have taken to write this, I think Brendan may be on the much more lucrative hourly rate.

One of the basic principles of Japanese design is that one should "eschew any decoration that is not integral to structure." I'm not sure I am coming close to adhering to the most austere interpretation of this, but it does help me make some decisions. Brendan asked whether I wanted to add a horizontal strip of green trim at the top of the wall against the bamboo soffits. The bamboo itself looked good against the side panels, but then so too did the piece of trim he held in place. Applying the principle of eschewing needless decoration made it easy to choose to not add the trim.

My role in building now seems reduced to Brendan occasionally shouting up the stairs to where I'm typing this, telling me, as earlier today, that he'll soon run out of bamboo. He needs four more poles, he thinks. So I save my text, scoot down to the car, and am greeted increasingly cheerfully by my friends at the landscape supply yard. I open the passenger-side rear window and two guys come to help slide the bamboo delicately into the front passenger leg space. That leaves about six feet sticking out in the cold breeze. After paying and discussing the merits of bamboo for soffits, I tie a red flag to the end of the bamboo and negotiate the heavy traffic; unless I give my poles appropriate leeway, they are ready to scrape buses and trucks, or to take out the occasional tall loiterer at bus stops.

Finishing the interior

This morning began with Brendan adding some caulking around the exterior and me cleaning up the interior prior to putting in insulation. Brendan decided that we might be able to get the insulation and dry wall in place by the end of the day. I began with the remainder of the thick insulation I had used in the base, tearing it in half then cutting it to fit between the studs. When I had used it all up, I came in to make Brendan some tea. The phone rang. A friend wanted to know if I would be swimming today, as I usually do before lunch. I explained that I had a cold and was anyway in a hurry to get the insulation in, and I was just going to get another bale of the stuff. He said he had an unused bale, and would I like it?

After I drove round to his place and put the bale in the back of the car, I asked whether I could pay him for it.

"Let's say that if ever I need a bale of insulation in the future, you owe me one. Otherwise, it's yours."

This seemed a very civilized way of proceeding, so I thanked him, listened with some foreboding to his woeful story of trying and failing to contain runaway bamboo, sympathized with him because his cat insisted on walking all over his car as soon as he'd washed it—the muddy evidence being only too evident—recommended the solutions people had offered me to keep raccoons away from the fish—from land mines to motion-sensitive water jets—sped back home, and started stuffing his kindly donated insulation between the remaining studs.

There is something wonderfully satisfying about insulating with these packs of fluffy fiberglass. They slot in so neatly and promise future coziness at small present cost. They must be disobeying one of the laws of nature or of Murphy. My friend's bale was bright yellow, whereas the one I had put up earlier had been bright pink. The combination looks like a toy maker's fantasy.

Colored insulation.

We were still a bit short of insulation to finish the ceiling area. I drove off to get some more, while Brendan began on the dry wall. By the time I got back, he was halfway round the interior. He graciously acknowledged that, there being so little room, I might be better off writing this than getting in his way—not that he put it like that. He did allow me to help with an awkward piece of dry wall that was to fit above the door and window up to the central 4" × 4" from which the rafters hung. As I lifted it in place, he whipped his cordless screwdriver from its holster and zapped in half a dozen dry-wall screws in seconds. I find the unhurried ease impressive, and also the speed at which it allows the professional to work. I too work unhurriedly, but the results, alas, are just slowness and something far from ease.

Risking his wife's wrath, Brendan says he will come over in the morning tomorrow, which is Saturday, to paste the first layer of joint compound over the taped joints of the dry wall.

The last week
I must put the text of this chapter and the next and the Conclusion (the latter two already written) in the mail a week from tomorrow, the last Monday of February, if I am to meet my editor's deadline. Brendan did put on the paste yesterday, and will be here in the morning to sand it. At the moment a humidifier and heater are going all weekend to dry everything out, so that we can prime the walls as soon as the dry wall is smooth.

To finish, we need to put 1" × 6" cedar planks on the ceiling, then tack bamboo strips across them, and perhaps cover the 4" × 4" at the peak of the ceiling with bamboo as well. The rear wall I intend to cover with a paper print designed for *fusuma* sliding doors—I will buy door "skins" and glue the print onto them and mount them on the wall. The alcove will be painted black, maybe, and the other walls will be a light earth color with a hint of green—back to my paint-associate friends and the infinite shades of beige. Wood trim around the room will be fir. Once the ceiling and walls are taken care of, it will be time for the tatami mats to go down, and we will build a fir frame all around the room between the walls and the tatami. In the alcove, I imagine a seat-high fir base, on which I will put a cushion for sitting, or, as one of the books assures me, I can compose "modest displays" in it—a hanging, with perhaps an off-center vase and a single and simple plant or a bare and interesting branch. Then after finishing the interior, the last job is to put in decking, build steps down to the lawn, and finish the balcony.

If all this gets done in a week, it will be a miracle. Today, Sunday, was unseasonably warm, so I went out to play around with stain. I wanted to try staining the supports of the structure green instead of black, and to begin putting on a final coat, touching up pieces that had been battered a little during the construction and covering the beads of white caulking Brendan had traced around the windows and trim.

To do this, I had to reconstruct the temporary scaffold I had seen Brendan put up last week. I used more nails than perhaps were necessary, and then slid the heavy 2" × 8" plank across the supports from the sides of the teahouse to the railings of the balcony. I heaved myself up, then I climbed down again, remembering to put the can of stain on the plank first. Then back onto the plank and the small matter of carefully getting to my feet, holding on to pieces of trim as I slowly did so. The pond seemed a long way down, and somehow anticipatory, the goldfish ready to take cover as I came in to join them. The plank was stretched across a ten-foot gulf from one support to the other, and bounced like a springboard as I moved.

Surprisingly, I got the staining done, put nearly all of it onto the wood and not onto me, and didn't tumble into the pond. I think, for the final coat, I will ask my paint associates to add some brown to the stain, to make it a little more subdued. At the moment the exterior of the teahouse/study looks positively cheerful. Considering the product of the afternoon's work, just to ensure that Murphy's law reaps its usual obedience, I concluded that black is indeed better than green for the structural supports, so need to redo some of what I have done this afternoon.

❡ Monday ❡ Brendan put the alcove window frames in, and told me that the place he was getting the glass from had suffered some crucial machine breakdown, and they were backordered. He then went to work with interior trim around the windows, cutting the fir to make an austerely handsome frame such as we'd seen in one of the books. For the last part of the day he was laying another band of paste over the joints and holes in the dry wall.

He had told me that he had once worked with a guy who was a dry-wall wizard who had developed a method of pasting dry wall without creating any dust. He worked slowly, though. Brendan smiled. This seemed miraculous to me, as a feature of dry-walling was sanding the hardened joint compound, and getting the white dust over everything. I imagined this guy as some ancient European craftsman, looking like Max von Sydow.

My jobs involved getting more bamboo. I now know the contents of the bamboo racks in the landscape supply shed rather better than do any of the employees. I got a single four-inch piece, twelve feet long, to finish off under the eaves, and ten thinner more uniformly yellow pieces for the inside ceiling. Returning with these, I then put a layer of paint on the small molding Brendan had cut to surround the delayed glass on the exterior of the alcove windows. My next job, after making tea and cookies for Brendan, was to select the paint for the interior walls at the local hardware store.

When I returned and was carrying bamboo to the back of the garden, a cheap and battered car pulled into the driveway. I assumed it was a visitor for one of the young men next door, across our shared drive. A thin, pale, and rather scruffy youth, with undecided facial hair, emerged and smiled vaguely in my direction. He hung around a minute, then came toward our gate.

"I'm a friend of Brendan's."

"Ah, he's back in the teahouse."

"It's coming along." He spoke as though he had been here before.

I dropped the bamboo by the pond, then came into the house to begin typing, but was concerned, finding the youth's behavior a bit odd. He seemed to spend much of his time standing on the lawn making notes in a small book. I began developing fantasies; perhaps he was the "legs" for some protection racket that was skimming money off tradesmen like Brendan, calculating what he could afford from this job for the big guy downtown. Or perhaps he was the editor of the carpenters' newsletter, soliciting a piece for their regular monthly column on "madmen I have worked for." Later, after he'd left, I went out to discuss some item of tomorrow's likely attack on the ceiling.

Brendan was up on a raised plank putting another covering of paste on the dry-wall joints.

"That was the dry-wall wizard I was telling you about. He was showing me how to get a perfect finish without creating any dust. You need this special kind of cloth and bunch it up really hard, wet it, and immediately after laying on the mud — the paste — you slide the cloth over it. I thought I'd give it a try."

❧ Tuesday ❧ The day began with the news that the lumberyard was out of the 1" × 6" cedar planks we were planning to put on the ceiling. They will pick some up during the day and have them ready for tomorrow morning. I have to attend a meeting beginning about midday—some holiday!—so won't be around to help today. Brendan planned to finish off some bits on the exterior before doing a final cleanup of the drywall paste, but his resolve was shaken by the ominous clouds behind the house, which turned into a deluge half an hour later.

We spent a little time inside the teahouse holding against the fir trim these tiny strips of color I picked up yesterday from the paint store. My problem with these is that I am influenced as much by their names as by the colors, so might find myself selecting Indian Peach, Green Summer, Woodbine, Sunnybrook Yellow, Orion, Amish Linen, County Cork, Mayan Gold, or Kenya Coral for their names and associations rather than for how well they would suit the interior walls.

It doesn't seem fair that Brendan gets all the good jobs and I am a dogsbody. There he is, with his admittedly vastly superior skills and tools, cutting the fir trim with professional precision, trying out new techniques for dealing with joint compound, cutting the cedar for the ceiling and mounting it. I get to crouch in the basement putting another coat of paint around the exterior trim, oiling the cedar before it goes onto the ceiling, and tidying up now and then. I hate painting, and that's all I'm allowed to do, apart from running errands.

One of the fun things he got to do while I was away was shape the piece of four-inch bamboo to fit the remaining space under the eaves. One of the women at the meeting I was at today is Korean, and she has a lively interest in and extensive knowledge of Japanese gardens, teahouses, and Zen. I worry that my compromising approach might be something of a scandal to Heesoon, but she takes it in good spirit. I mentioned that I had an alcove, and she agreed that this was a tad presumptuous of me. I also mentioned that in some of the books I had seen, a prominent corner of the alcove is fitted with either a bared part of a tree trunk or with bamboo. She assured me that it is indeed almost a requirement that some untreated but beautiful natural material serve such a purpose. Heesoon looked at the color samples I had with me, not entirely by chance. She felt that green would be better than some of the beiges I was considering. One of her daughters, Serenne, came in with a moss garden in a bowl. She had five or six different kinds of moss growing, which was quite an accomplishment, as each required somewhat different light and moisture conditions. Among the bowl's green mounds was a small tuft of the kind I had used in my moss gardens, and so I learned that it was called star moss. (Serenne and her sister, Lumina, had scoured a beach on Haida Gwaii — Queen Charlotte Islands — collecting black stones for the stream bed between the bog and the pond.)

When I returned home, I mentioned to Brendan that it was desirable, if not obligatory, to put a piece of bamboo around the corner of the alcove. The remaining piece of the handsome bronzed four-inch bamboo he had used under the eaves was just enough to fit perfectly on the corner.

❧ Wednesday ❧   The day began with my buying paint for the walls and Danish oil for the cedar that is to go on the ceiling. I got back to find that Brendan had arrived with the cedar and was set up sanding it in the driveway. He sanded, then I brushed off any remaining sawdust and rolled oil into the boards. It is always an aesthetic delight and something of a miracle to see the cedar come to its varied colored life as soon as the oil begins to soak in.

Over lunch we chatted about the culture of carpenters, dwelling on his horror stories about, for example, the crooks who search out older widows to work for, ripping them off at every turn, and also the carpenters who get ripped off after doing elaborate jobs. We agreed that it was a terrible world out there and decided that we would go together the follow-

ing morning to pick up the tatami mats, lamps, sandals, a cushion, and the fusuma panels.

As the proprietor of the Japanese products place is there
only by appointment, I phoned. He said he could be there at
10 A.M. I was about to hang up when he said, "Cash only sale."

"I can't use a Visa or check?"

"No. Cash only."

"How much does it all add up to then?"

"I have to calculate. I call you back."

Brendan and I wondered whether I might ask if there was
a discount for people who worked for the tax authorities.
Another effect of this call has been my going back through
this chapter to find the proprietor's name and changing it, to
protect the possibly guilty. So "Mr. Lee" is not called Mr. Lee.
And a further effect was a visit to the bank to ask for $1,300
cash from our already overdrawn account. (*Surely* you can think
of people for whom this book would make a perfect present?)

While I finished off oiling the cedar planks, Brendan went
out with his special cloth to finish the final pasting and scraping of the dry wall, hoping to get a coat of primer on the walls
before the end of the day. But he had to leave early, so that's
a job for the morning.

❈ Thursday ❈ Brendan began by priming the whole of the
interior, and then we set off to see "Mr. Lee." The drive across
town involved pleasant chatting about recent jobs, including
one on a steep hillside on the north shore: an expensive house
under which a stream ran, exposed under glass beside a wide
stairway. It sounded like a knockoff of Frank Lloyd Wright's
Fallingwater house. The $40,000 renovation ended up cost-
ing the owners over $100,000, as rot and shoddy work were
exposed once the surface materials were removed.

"But they were both lawyers, so it didn't faze them."

Mr. Lee seemed to be involved in an altercation with some-

The ceiling against our garden fence, oiled and ready to mount. The teahouse is at the back of the garden behind this stack.

one on the street as we arrived, though they parted amicably as he came across to join us. I was discouraged to think that this might be his normal style of bargaining. Inside, Brendan poked around, examining the examples of Mr. Lee's woodworking, and looking through the impressive portfolio of work he had done. Not, surely, all on a cash basis? The tatami mats were boxed ready to go, and we gathered together the rest of my loot. An additional item I was persuaded to buy was one of those legless chairs and a splendid red cushion.

During the afternoon, Brendan fastened the cedar planks to the rafters, and laid strips of bamboo across them to make a dramatic and beautiful ceiling. In the basement, I was doing more painting and had a very strange thing happen. Clumsily opening a new can of paint, I dropped the lid onto the basement floor, and it fell paint side up!

Brendan left a bit early, as it was his wife's birthday. While we were driving back from Mr. Lee's, he had said that he wouldn't be able to come tomorrow, as he had another job he needed to attend to. I also had a meeting tomorrow, so I assumed nothing would happen till next week. But the woodwork in the teahouse/study went so well this afternoon, and looks so good, that Brendan said he would phone and explain that he wouldn't be able to make it to the other job tomorrow. Instead he would come here and finish off the remaining pieces of trim around the windows. Over the weekend I will paint, then we can put down the tatami mats, build the fir frame around them, wire up the shoji lamps, and be within striking distance of finishing the interior.

❧ Friday ❧ At the end of the day I returned to find that Brendan had finished the woodwork. On the way home, I had bought paint for the walls, in shades of green, as Heesoon had recommended. In the end, after a frothing dither of indecisiveness, I bought a lightish green for the walls and a dark green for the alcove. Feeling insecure about the decisions, I bought only sample-sized cans.

❧ Saturday ❧ My wife and I spent the morning babysitting Joshua and Jordan, and by the time I got out to the teahouse/study, I had time only to put a couple of coats of varnish on the fir with which Brendan had trimmed the windows and door.

❧ Sunday ❧ I needed to do some paperwork in the morning; pay bills, delay bills, avoid bills—that kind of thing. Then I put a layer of the dark green paint in the alcove. It looked too bright at first, but darkened and deepened as it dried. I had enough of the sample of the lighter paint to get about half of the walls covered. It's not the paint's fault, I know it is doing its best; but as I sat on the floor looking at the wall opposite, I concluded that I had chosen a too light and rather boring green, almost a pastel. I think I will have to go to the paint shop in the morning and ask for a deeper, more interesting color, and perhaps have the young woman there add some black to the dark green.

❧ Monday ❧   As 2000 is a leap year, I have a day more than I had calculated to get the text to the editor. But, starting the day by taking a look at yesterday's painting, I was convinced that the light green just didn't work. Since I had covered half the interior with it, I tried very hard to convince myself that it was just great, but in the end skulked off to the paint shop for something to replace it.

The young woman behind the counter takes color seriously. Her hair is a bright three-toned confection in orange and red with a straw-yellow strand across the top. It actually looks quite good and is certainly more arresting than last Friday's brown. I spent some time with my eyes sliding gloomily across the color samples. Nothing seemed remotely right. I felt that perhaps there were somewhere important colors that they had forgotten to display, colors that were just right for the tea-house/study. But the paper samples on display seemed to cover the usual spectrum. My color seemed always to be between samples.

I approached the counter with best guesses and the copy of *A Japanese Touch for Your Home* book. She had a quick eye, flicking expertly through her thick fan of samples and finding better matches for the pictures of walls I indicated.

"I think that's it," she said authoritatively. Each of the color samples had a number. "I've always liked 534. It has depth and color, light but muscular."

I thought I'd put her in touch with a few wine-freaks I know.

"I think you'll find 534 does the job for you. That 431 you chose last week is more like a children's bedroom, or perhaps a conservatory wall. It's sprightly and lighthearted, but doesn't have the depth or energy of 534."

I bought a gallon, and she was right. I was halfway round the interior again when Brendan turned up. He had had to go to that other job this morning, and had hoped I might have the painting finished so he could get the floor in. I described my follies in paint choice. He agreed to take over finishing the painting while I came in to have a late lunch and write up this morning's small adventure of paint buying. He can't come tomorrow, so on Wednesday, after I put a second coat on, we will get the floor done, and the tatami mats down.

The week after the last week

Quite suddenly, it seems, the remaining items have been finished one by one. These have been what Brendan calls "high-production days." The best professional work, one slowly realizes, is mostly preparation. The highly visible finishing takes relatively little time—but how it looks is almost entirely a result of the care and quality of the less visible preparatory work that seems to take forever.

In the kitchen I have been accumulating a bowl of tea leaves. After making Brendan's tea each day, and my own, I toss the tea bags on one side, and later break them open and put the used leaves into the bowl. When the painting was finished, I took the damp tea leaves out and spread them around the floor. This allows me to sweep up the accumulated mess from dry wall and wood and dirty shoes without the dust flying around. There seems a poetic appropriateness in using the tea leaves we have enjoyed in this way. It's a trick I learned as a Franciscan novice long ago when sweeping cloisters.

With the floor clean, Brendan built the fir surrounds for the tatami mats. Once begun, he scoured my basement where I, jackdaw-like, keep leftover wood from past household projects. He needed bits of thin plywood to build up the floor under the fir so that it would be exactly the same level as the mats.

The next day, while Brendan was away at another job, I put a couple of coats of varnish on the fir. He came back as I was precariously up the ladder adding a final coat of Danish oil to the cedar ceiling. I had at first been careful not to get the oil on the strips of bamboo that spanned the ceiling. But Brendan started running an oil-impregnated cloth over the bamboo, and it too gleamed richly. The ceiling looks so good I might spend much of my time in the teahouse/study on my back looking up.

I had to go back to the job I am paid to do, leaving Brendan to deal with the final wiring of the lights and the heater. I had assumed that a baseboard heater would be best, but regretted that it would stick out into the room, given that I had so little space, and wanted to keep it as uncluttered as possible. Brendan mentioned that one could get a heater that slotted in between the studs, with just a grill visible mounted on the wall. I got one when coming home from work, and he had it mounted the next day.

Each day, when I came home after Brendan had left, the project seemed to be magically growing toward completion. The shoji lights were in place, the heater was in and working, the ceiling and floor were finished, the alcove with its corner piece of bamboo was ready.

After some final touchup painting, with the fir dry, I slid the tatami mats into place, and took out the black legless chair and the glamorous scarlet cushion. The chair and cushion looked so good that I phoned Mr. Lee and bought a second set. All that the interior needed now was a desk in front of the window. Brendan would make shoji screens for the win-

A legless chair on the tatami mats.

dows after finishing the one remaining large-scale job of building the balcony and its railing.

Mike arrived from Japan, bringing the gutter buckets and a wall hanging. Brendan nailed up the pieces of six-inch bamboo as gutters, one on either side of the teahouse, cut a hole and strung the set of buckets under them. I will get a couple of half-barrels into which they will drain. Rainwater falls from bucket to bucket down the chain. At the bottom is a wider heavy bucket to prevent the chain being blown too far in the

Legless chairs and tasseled cushions by the alcove.

The chain of minibuckets, viewed through the circle of laminated slices of mahogany that Brendan made.

wind. Instead of the half-barrels, Mike suggested digging a hole, burying a bronze or ceramic bowl, and covering the opening with stones. Water falling into it through the stones should make a magic echoing sound.

The balcony

The last item to be added was the balcony. One of the continuing doubts I have had since beginning the teahouse/study has been the wood to use for the deck. It is three feet by ten feet. My preference, all other things, like cost, being equal, which they aren't, would be for jarrah. This is partly a sentimental choice, but also aesthetic. I have visited western Australia a few times, and have been astonished by gorgeous jarrah floors in some of the older houses. It is a rich red-brown. Jarrah trees were grown almost exclusively in southwest Australia. I remember a delightful trip down to Margaret River, and seeing parts of the twenty-by-one-hundred-mile strip in which the jarrah mainly grew. At the time I visited, there was a crisis because a blight was threatening to ravage the forest. It seems that some fungus had been brought into the area on the treads of huge machines used in mining bauxite.

A fancy woodworking store carried tongue-and-groove jarrah, and some time ago said they might be able to get boards for a deck. Apparently, they sold it mostly to people building expensive yachts. It would cost about $600 to do the deck and steps. Then they phoned back to say they couldn't get it. Then, recently, I stopped into another branch of the same place, and was told that they could get it. I had more or less agreed with Brendan that we would do the deck in mahogany, but told him that jarrah might be available. We agreed the price made it pretty prohibitive, but he said that he knew where they were probably getting it from, and one of the managers there used to work for him. Heh, heh. He also said that he had never worked the wood and would very much like to.

I visited the huge sheds of another supplier of specialty woods, and mentioned to one of the guys that I was looking for jarrah.

"Don't know about that. You should see George in the office. But have a look around if you want."

There was a balcony on both sides of the shed, so I climbed up one side and looked at the massive planks of unfinished exotic hardwoods, from forests in Central and South America, southeast Asia, some few from Africa, and seemingly every steaming jungle in the galaxy. As I ambled by, doing the equivalent of kicking the tires, stroking and hefting planks, I asked the passing employees about particular woods, receiving the almost invariable answer, "You should ask George about that."

After an intoxicating while, I found the office and did indeed ask George. I was fortunate to get to him, as apparently everyone entering the place was told to see George. He was exactly what you might expect: a solid, salt-of-the-earth sixty-year-old who had been involved with exotic woods from close to birth. I mentioned that I was planning a small deck and was looking for jarrah. This was the right kind of thing to say. His air of slightly harried busyness lifted in a moment; he smiled at the thought of jarrah, and gave me his full attention. We talked for a while of the beauties of jarrah, and of the project for which I wanted it.

"We don't have planks at the moment. You won't find any in the city. If you want a red wood, you might try bubinga or padauk."

"I've never heard of either of them."

"Ask one of the boys to show you. They're up on the right. The bubinga would set you back . . ."—he did some calculations—". . . about, well, you won't see much change from a thousand. The padauk we could get a bit cheaper."

I took a look at them, but didn't feel any special affinity to these beautiful, exotic, and costly woods, and thought that maybe the dream of jarrah would have to be forgone. Perhaps if I'd spent time in the steamy heat of Malaysian forests where the red-sapped and red-brown wooded padauk came from, I'd want it for my deck, and perhaps it was the visits to the vineyards around Margaret River that made the jarrah trees so romantically memorable. My one visit to Malaysia led me to believe that the only flora left were palm trees. I drove north from Singapore through endless miles of unvarying palms. Thirty years earlier it might have seemed that the place grew nothing but rubber-yielding trees. With the invention of artificial rubber, the vast plantations, which had begun with trees imported from Brazil, had been wiped out and replaced with the palms, which now generate for Malaysia the world's greatest production of palm oil. (I was thinking how Anthony Burgess would have found this so alien, despite his years here. Remembering, too, from his *The Long Day Wanes* [New York: Norton, 1993] all those Tiger beers drunk in a vain attempt to fight the desiccating heat. I had some Tigers in his memory under the fans on the Long Bar at Raffles in Singapore.)

In the end, I settled for Honduran mahogany. It cost a bit more than other kinds, but has a tight grain, is hard and strong, and once oiled it is a gorgeous rich brown. Far too beautiful to let anyone stand on. Brendan used that new system of screwing the boards in place from underneath so that the top of the wood is unmarked by nails. The result is stunning.

I tried some sketches for the railings, and as we had quite a lot of the bamboo used on the ceiling of the teahouse left over, we decided to incorporate that into the design. Then we decided on a design Mike drew. Then I remembered that I had some mahogany, bought years ago, in the basement, and perhaps we could make the rails from that. Brendan, Mike, and I stood sketching possibilities for the railings, looking for something that would create an authentic Japanese feel. It was hard not to be bemused by the oddity of three Irishmen in

The deck and railings in place.

western Canada struggling to articulate visions of Japanese tea-house railings.

We finally chose a design from a picture of a nineteenth-century Japanese post office. I found it on a pamphlet from the extraordinary Meiji-Mura Museum outside Nagoya. Meiji-Mura (Meiji Village) is unlike any museum I have ever seen. It covers about one million square meters and is made up of about sixty buildings from the Meiji period (1868–1912). Dr. Tanigushi and Mr. Tsuchikawa, who had been boyhood friends, were distressed at the increasing destruction, by fire, war, earthquake, and, not least, by development, of the great buildings of the period. They bought this huge swath of land overlooking Lake Iruka, selected the finest buildings that were in danger of destruction, and had them disassembled and rebuilt in their museum. (The word "museum" derives from the Greek Muses, and so the use of the word for this collection

The deck and steps.

of gorgeous buildings is entirely appropriate.) Among the buildings saved from destruction is the entrance and central portion of the magnificent Frank Lloyd Wright Imperial Hotel, brought from Tokyo.

Brendan took the mahogany home with him to cut and replicate the design in his workshop. We stained the wood a couple of times, with Mike putting on a final coat, and then Brendan nailed them into place—and the teahouse/study was finished.

nine

Finishing as spring comes again

THERE SEEM TO BE A THOU-
sand things still to do, or at least to get the garden into a condition from which . . . well, what do I mean? I was going to
say that I would finish and then there would be just routine
pottering, that there comes an indefinite and indistinct time
when one moves from making to maintaining. But there is no
finishing point because there is always something to add or
change to take the garden closer to the foolish heart's desire.
It is only our stories that have beginnings and endings. Nature
doesn't recognize our starts and finishes, but just carries on
around us, heartless and storyless. We are the story makers,
and so, athwart nature, I am going to come to a finish when
I have the overall shape of the garden more or less fitting the
vague notion I began with.

Spring, at least, is punishingly reliable, but I wasn't so sure
I had done the right things to enable it to do what I hope for
the bamboo. The thin-stemmed and small specimens I had
planted certainly hadn't died, but perhaps the soil or the placement or the water barrier might in some ways combine to stunt
their growth. I kept looking for signs of new culms bursting
from the ground, but nothing showed. I talked to people in

nurseries, some of whom assured me they should be up by now, and others reassured me that they still had time. I was almost ready to take the Walkman out to play Mozart to them, when, one morning, there were suddenly half a dozen thumb-thick pointed culms already inches above ground. Within days, the tallest was over a foot high. I had read about the speed with which bamboo grew, but this was ludicrous. Within a few more days, they were shoulder height, and then above my head and making for the clouds. And then, quite suddenly, they stopped, about the level of the top of the fence. Perhaps next year the new culms will go higher.

Between the raised garden, pond, and fence, where the bamboo is now growing vigorously from each of its three containers (I *hope* they will contain it!), I can now finally lay down a covering of stones. I go back to one of my favorite places, the landscape supply yard.

I had earlier bought some dark blue/gray stones as samples and decided they were what I wanted. But nothing is easy. Here next to them were wide tubs of stones in colors I hadn't seen before. Particularly attractive was a dark tan stone, which was called "red Mexican pebbles." Alongside it were "purple Mexican pebbles," "black Mexican pebbles," and "tequila sunrise pebbles." The black was what I imagined getting, but I filled a couple of bags with the red as well, just to lay them against the fence to see whether some magic confluence might strike. The pebbles I had were a half inch to one inch in size—though many were bigger than that—but here was a tub of two-inch black pebbles, and perhaps they might work better along the fence. So I added a bag of those as well.

Inside the office area I asked a new young man behind the counter if he knew where the various stones came from. I had a notebook, so mentioned that I was writing a book about my little building project and hoped to add some background to the items I was buying. He didn't know and called up the

New bamboo culms.

stairs behind him, which led to a balcony where the yard manager had his office. The laconic man I had dealt with a few
times before looked down unsmilingly. In all my visits he had
maybe spoken a dozen words, of the yes/no/over there/check
or Visa? variety. I was interested in the black Mexican pebbles
and had to begin with the question that would mark me as an
idiot, but tried to soften the blow by asking:

"I assume they come from Mexico?"

He lowered his elbows onto the ledge of the balcony and
his face relaxed into what might count as close to a smile.

"There's a beach. Miles long. Endless stones of all colors.
They've been stripping it for twenty years. A guy or family
buys the rights to a section of beach and they sort the stones
by hand—colors, sizes, shapes, quality. Imagine the day. Down
to the beach with the family, even the kids get a bag each.
With your own kind of stone to find." He stopped, or seemed
to pause, but didn't begin again.

"Do you get them direct from Mexico?"

"No. Supplier in San Diego."

I came home with bags of the red stone and of the larger
black stone. Wheelbarrowing them to the rear of the garden,
and tipping them against sections of the fence, I realized immediately that both were mistakes. The reds were too bright. I had
thought they might be a good continuation of the reddish-
brown balcony decking. And the black stones were too big.
Heigh-ho. The small black ones were right all along. I should
have remembered the principle from one of the books I had
consulted—"small fish, small stones." I assume this doesn't mean
I will have to upgrade the size of my stones as the fish grow.

Of course, I was convinced of this only after I had spread
all the stones I had brought home on top of the compacted
gravel. The next day I faced the chore of gathering all the
stones and getting them back into the bags. Knees and back
complained again, as well they might. Then I discovered that

the tire on my wheelbarrow had given up the ghost. What had been a slow leak had become a total deflation, and it let air out as fast as I was pumping it in. Now how was I to get the stones to the car? Recently I had bought one of those trashcans on wheels, so forced it into reluctant service. It was obvious that it thought hauling heavy bags of stone across the lawn was not at all its kind of work, but, complaining and digging its small wheels into the lawn here and there, it did the job.

Back at the landscape supply center, the laconic manager was happy to accept back these stones, and swap them for five bags of the small Mexican black pebbles. By this point my knees were creaking, and I happily accepted the help of the young man who came out to show me where to return the old stones and where to get the smaller black pebbles. They were in bags, straight from the Mexican beach, via San Diego, under the awning next to the shed in which the pond liner had been cut, or miscut, some months before, and in which the familiar bags of Chinese bamboo rested.

"This is my last job of the day," he cheerily told me.

In front of the tightly piled bags there was an area of oily mud, a couple of inches deep at its center. We tried to avoid it, climbing onto the piles to find the bags with the pebble size I wanted. Taking the easier part, I tossed the bags forward for him to pick up and load into the back of the car. He hopped up onto the front pile to get the last bag and began to step down holding it.

You know those moments when you can see something happening before it happens, but don't have time to say or do anything even though everything seems to be moving in such slow motion you could play a game of cricket in the time it took? The bags of stone were shipped from San Diego in sets of about fifty in heavy-plastic sheathing, which had been cut through to allow access to individual bags. At the front, the plastic hung in a loop just below the level of the top bags. The young man caught his foot in this loop on the way down, falling forward directly into the inches of oily mud.

He lay for a moment, rising without any evident damage except mud all over his pants and sleeves. The bag of stones, onto which he had fallen, had saved the front of his coat.

"Well, that was my last job for the day," he said good-humoredly, but not quite as cheerfully as a few minutes earlier. I drove home with the bags, a little guilty that he had borne the cost of loading them. They were so heavy that I had to climb into the trunk of the car to toss them out onto the driveway.

Before I could get them to the back of the garden, I needed to get the wheel of my barrow fixed. At the bicycle shop about 10 A.M. the following morning I was greeted by an unshaven guy eating a sandwich. Early lunch, or perhaps a late and unconventional breakfast?

"This is a bike shop," he accused me, pointing at the squat wheel I was carrying.

"I ride a very small fat bicycle," I said.

"We've had a run on these wheelbarrow wheels recently. I've fixed three of them in about two years. So I'm really good at it now."

I wasn't encouraged, though this Monty Pythonesque exchange was more fun than the usual politenesses. He grabbed the wheel, switching sandwich and wheel a couple of times as he led me energetically to the back of the shop. After trying to pump compressed air in for five seconds, he said:

"The seal's shot. You'll need to get an inner tube. Try the lumberyard or the tool rental place across the street."

Warily, I entered the tool rental shop, concerned that I would be told I needed a hovercraft for the job, not a wheelbarrow. With some relief, I saw that my friend who always insisted I needed something other than what I asked for was just leaving.

"Ted'll take care of you," he said. And Ted did, in minutes putting in a tube, blowing it up, and sending me back to trundle the stones to the rear of the garden, and pour them out around the bamboo and against the fence. They were exactly right. But I still needed, I calculated, about another eight bags. After another visit to the landscape supply yard, and spreading the further eight bags along the fence, I decided I still needed a further four.

I thought this might be my last visit to the supply yard and its paradise of stones, and felt almost nostalgic. My laconic manager greeted me cheerfully.

"More Mexican black?"

"Four more bags should see the end, and about six or seven basalt wall stones to give an edge for them."

"Okay. I'll have one of the guys load the stones for you, then you drive onto the weighscale, make a note of what the car weighs, then pile in what you need of the wall stones, back onto the scale, and we charge you for the difference."

With the stones in the trunk, I drove onto the weigh machine, which announced in red lighted numbers that I weighed 4,050 pounds. I then backed to the piles of basalt and loaded in enough to complete a small wall round the side of the teahouse, irritated that I had forgotten my work gloves and was getting grime from the stones on my leather town gloves. The idea was to make a small wall separating the Mexican black pebbles from the gravel under the teahouse. I would have liked to continue the pebbles to the rear fence and under the teahouse, but to do that I would have to take out another mortgage. I had already spilled around $500 worth of a Mexican beach into my garden. No doubt the Mexican family that laboriously selected and packed the stones made about $10.

With the basalt in the car I now weighed 4,220 pounds. How much would I have to pay for those few stones? Weren't they some significant amount a pound? I was trying to calculate what this was going to cost as I walked back into the office where my laconic friend was poised over a calculator. "4,050 in and 4,220 out," I said, still trying to calculate. "Can that be right? That seems a lot of pounds for the few stones I put in the car."

I was puzzled that moving 170 pounds of stones was so easy.

"Well, you're a good customer, so I'll just call it 100 pounds."

"Oh no. No, I mean, I'm just interested to know whether I could have carried 170 pounds so easily. What, maybe 20 pounds to 30 pounds per stone. I see, of course, it could easily be 170 pounds."

But by this time he had entered my total as 100 pounds, and charged me only $12 for the basalt. I do well as an inadvertent bargainer.

I built a small curving continuation of the pond wall along the west side of the teahouse and around the back of the second set of bamboo. Then I poured the remaining stones inside the new wall. While setting the stones in place, I wasn't surprised to see that the culms of bamboo in the now hidden—except through the teahouse window—set toward the rear corner were by far the sturdiest and blackest, and those most visible behind the pond were the weakest and most mottled. Perhaps another spring may change this.

Tuning the music of the waterfall

One feature of the garden I had intended to come back to was the waterfall into the pond. A waterfall's harmonics need careful attention if it is to create peace in the minds of its hearers. I had tried to improve its music when I fixed the overflow caused by my loading too many stones in the stream, but the flow of water was still too concentrated. It fell in a rush, creating a noise that had disturbing undertones of hurry and anxiety. I spent a careful hour or so, moving stones on the top of

The Mexican black pebbles.

the falls, altering the siting of the rocks, spreading the water out over the flat rock at the edge where the unsuspecting water found itself unsupported, dispersing the spray across more of the rocks on the way down, and ensuring greater diversity in the set of rivulets that splattered the pond.

Silly of me to think the water might not expect the sudden drop. It does nothing all day, every day, but settle for a while in the pond, get sucked into the pump, rush up the dark narrow hose to the bottom of the bog—and heaven knows what it's like down there—rise up through the stones, and emerge from the gravel into the light and air for the brief run down the stream to that familiar dive back into the pond.

After I had spent an hour or more fiddling with the stones, the water sounded as though it was not rushing, but was making more cheerful, many-toned, lighter, more diverse music.

Protecting the fish

Once the teahouse balcony was in place, it was difficult to remove and replace the chicken-wire frames I had built to protect the pond from raccoons and herons. I needed to come up with some other solution. Brendan had worked on a project where the owner had installed one of those motion sensor devices that triggered jets of water shooting in all directions around the pond. It was effective. But for that I would have to pipe water permanently out to the rear of the garden. Also I would have to lie in bed at night hearing the spray lashing every wandering cat and squirrel in the neighborhood. And I would have to live with the constant problem of ensuring it was switched off when our grandchildren decided to take a totter down the garden, or my wife and I ambled romantically down to the pond in the cool of a summer evening. Motion sensor spraying seemed likely to cause more problems than it might solve.

I had already dismissed my son's land-mine option. Someone said that most pond owners simply accepted that they had to "restock" the pond at regular intervals. Apart from the cost, I found this a distasteful way of thinking about my good friends the fish. They weren't merely decorative commodities, they were, as St. Francis would have called them, brothers and sisters, with their own fishy sensibilities.

A friend suggested a single large chicken-wire frame that I could lower from the front of the pond. At the moment there are three frames. Two measure four feet by eight feet, and one is a smaller irregular shape that fits the garden end of the pond. The single frame could be twelve or fourteen feet long, he suggested, and maybe eight feet wide, made with light 1" × 2"s reinforced by two-inch strips of thin plywood. But where would I put such a monster once I had lifted it off the pond? We also discussed my idea of a roll of mesh—either chicken wire or fabric—that would fit under the deck when not in use, be stapled to the teahouse support posts, and then could be rolled out when protection was needed. The problem with this is that it would require two people. Also I wasn't sure how one could arrange it so that it wouldn't interfere with the marginal plants.

I had the notion that I would return to finish this section when I came up with a solution that would earn your admiration for its efficiency and ingenuity. But even though the old chicken-wire frames are difficult to maneuver into place, they are manageable and do the job. The ignominious end of this section is that I am having to settle for what I had at the beginning. If I come up with something better, I'll give a description of it on the Web site that accompanies this book (http://www.educ.sfu.ca/people/faculty/kegan/Japangarden home.html).

Brother donkey

St. Francis of Assisi, in the usual representation of him these days, appears to be something of a wimp, a symbol of a sentimental attachment to animals and flowers. But Francis Bernardone was a tough customer, rebellious and hard as nails. Toward the end of his life, he was told that he was going blind, and that the recommended remedy was to cauterize one of his eyes. When the glowing metal for the operation, without anesthetic, was taken red from the fire, he rose and greeted it with a friendly gesture, calmly saying: "Brother Fire, God made you beautiful and strong and useful; I pray you be courteous with me."

His fasting and sicknesses, and his ascetic life in general, led to his body becoming exhausted before he was fifty. He spent his astonishing energy prodigally, hauling along what he called Brother Donkey, his body. Well, this is perhaps an overwrought introduction to some minor observations about the wear and tear this project has wrought in my Brother Donkey. But St. Francis's semihumorous and semiaffectionate relationship with his body seems more appropriate than our usual coddling. Though we might find his ruthless disregard of its comforts daunting.

His was an attitude that shares something with Chuang Tzu's. As he was dying, his disciples said they would give him the most splendid burial. But Chuang Tzu said that he would prefer to have the heaven and earth for his coffin, the sun and moon, planets and constellations, as jewels around him. What more could he ask for than to stretch (as had St. Francis) on the cold ground? His disciples said they feared that the crows and kites would eat him. "Well," he said, "above ground I shall be eaten by crows and kites, below by ants and worms. In either case I shall be eaten. What have you got against birds?"

The project, at least, hasn't killed me. I did have thoughts that careless prancing around on the roof might have done for me, but Brendan took care of that. Early on, I managed to pull my back out a few times and was sent to a chiropractor. No doubt their cracking of backs is of some good to someone, but I couldn't detect any benefits from it. The back got better slowly whatever I did or didn't do for it. I did learn how to bend and lift large stones sensibly, except that seeing myself moving with care made me feel like an old man. Abusing the body seems a privilege of youth that brings age faster.

My much-operated-on knees—from a youth of soccer and other athletics—were the weak point in the project. They suffer from carrying weights. It became a matter of gauging how much I could manage one day so that they might recover overnight to allow me to manage a bit more the next. If I would have to go into the office on a following day, I could do a bit more work, and hobble a bit for the next days, till they recovered again. Only once did I overdo so much that I had to use a walking stick for a week.

As I look in the mirror after a shower, I guess some of the muscles are due to this project, though some of the other features seem to owe more to the tea and cookies. I seem to have managed to develop the muscles moderately well for the tasks I have faced, but have wrecked most of the joints in the process. I'd say these results suggest a straightforward design flaw in this model. The joints haven't caved in, they just cause pain. Everyone cheerfully assures me that the elbows will take more than a year to settle down, and the knees are beyond repair. Brother Donkey and I will have to do some physiotherapy stretched out on the tatami mats.

The pond water is very cold still, and the fish lethargically drift around at the bottom. But I have to lower the water lily from the shelf it has been resting on since I trimmed off the last of its decaying leaves and stems in the fall. It needs to be at the bottom of the pond, ready for its shoots to feel their way up to the surface when the water warms up. Getting the heavy pot down there will involve my lowering Brother Donkey into the water. It was all very well in the summer climbing in clad in swimming trunks, but I suspect such a maneuver now would have me in hospital suffering from exposure.

The solution seemed to be waders—thigh-high boots that strap over the shoulders. My wife favors this solution but giggles in a way I don't find encouraging as she suggests it. That she is also eager to take a photograph of me in waders worries me even more. I'm not sure what they represent in her mind, but seriousness and dignity clearly don't figure.

But where to get them? I assumed outdoor equipment shops would carry them, but my first couple of visits to such places resulted in frosty assurances that they did not carry such things. I was eventually directed, with some disapproval, to what I had assumed was just another outdoor equipment store. I learned that most people who buy waders seem to intend damage to living things—either fishing or shooting—and Mountain Equipment Co-op and such places greatly disapprove of these activities, and of people who want waders for just such nefarious purposes.

The store I was directed to was indeed decked out with just about everything you might need to kill fish, animals, or birds. The young men and women serving seemed all to be into self-mutilation as well, with studs in lips, noses, ears, and tongues, and a veritable gallery of tattoos. Leather and stained denim were the couture of choice. The young skinhead who served me was helpful and charming, and the female wrestler at the till pointed out that I could get a similar pair of waders for less, and one of the road-warriors in slit leather pants eagerly rushed off to replace the ones I had with their best deal.

I haven't yet had a chance to wade into the pond in these magnificent shiny-black artifacts, and am not altogether looking forward to it. I expect to slip, or have water trickle down over them. And how am I to avoid those watersnails I put into the pond a year ago and haven't seen since? Not a word of gratitude out of any of them. But the project is nearly finished, and Brother Donkey has survived well enough that my major concerns are some aching joints and a fear of getting cold water down my waders. It could have been a lot worse.

Cleaning up

Cleaning up after completing the interior of the tea-house/study involves finding a place for the leftover nails. We have used nearly twenty kinds of nails and screws on the project, from the massive galvanized carriage bolts that hold the base supports together down to tiny finishing nails that fasten the slim pieces of trim around the windows. There are the three-inch spikes used to construct the frame, and long green screws that secure the decking wood. As I sort the different kinds of nails and screws into glass jars, I am reminded of the job for which each was bought. But there are three or four whose use I can't even recall. Could they have been for building the fence, hauled out and not used in the teahouse/study? Here are dry-wall screws, shingle nails, exterior trim nails, and ah, those screws were what I used to fix the joists onto the support posts before putting the galvanized carriage bolts in. What a testament to the toolmaking ingenuity of our species.

(Incidentally, I put them in glass jars following a neat idea I had read about years ago. One screws the lid of the jar tightly to a joist or into the ceiling above one's workbench and then reaches up and screws the jar full of nails into its lid. Looking up one can see immediately what one has.)

Next I pile into a corner of the driveway all the remaining pieces of plywood, bits of trim and 2" × 4"s and 2" × 8"s, unused tarpaper, wire mesh, dry wall, slices of bamboo, bent nails, irregular and crumpled sheets of plastic, bent chunks of flashing, spare wisps of insulation, cracked shingles, blocks of 4" × 4" and 1" × 2" strips, unidentifiable slivers of wood, bits of plastic and metal, and a few twigs from shrubs that were caught up in the mayhem. As I toss down a chunk of plywood, I see Brendan has used it to take notes from calls on his cell phone. So I learn that Mrs. Stokes on Trafalgar Street wants her bathroom measured up on Friday, and on a spare piece of 2" × 4" he had a couple of phone numbers with "teak" next to one and "no mats" by the other.

The quince and the drooping strips

I think that I am clearing up after the garden is finished, but there are endless bits and pieces to deal with. Remember those 1" × 1" strips I mounted under the cap of the fence long ago? I had tried to persuade myself that the foot-long pieces I couldn't attach without their drooping were intended to droop.

This worked for a while, in that I carried on, leaving them like that, convincing myself that accepting their droop was bordering on a Zen insight. This conviction wavered a bit when a storm managed to tear a couple of them free. One fell in the next-door garden, which my fence had now made inaccessible without my trotting round the sidewalk. Though a new house is almost completed on that lot, the place is still uninhabited, and I was able to retrieve my bit of wood without too many odd looks from the array of workers swarming over the site. I would have to do something more radical to fix the strips in place.

The mahogany on the balcony railings looks really attractive, and I had a stack of four-foot pieces left over. Brendan suggested replacing the $1" \times 1"$ green strips with the red-brown stained mahogany, which would also serve to pull together the fence and teahouse. He drilled holes in the posts and carved the mahogany so that it fitted tightly into the holes.

You might also wonder about the outcome of the heroic struggle to transport the reluctant japonica quince from the next-door garden into my border of Mexican stones. I mentioned that the thriving part of the quince had been casually swept away and destroyed when they cleared the neighboring lot. Despite the liberated chunk languishing and dropping its leaves on my side, and standing like a bunch of dead twigs through the remainder of the year, now that spring has come again, the quince, as though in defiance of its near-death experience, has burst into prodigal red-pink blossom.

The teahouse was to be a study, and a study requires a desk and a chair. I had thought that perhaps I would buy these final items in a Japanese antiques shop. But I couldn't find anything suitable. I mentioned to Brendan that I had seen an attractive chair and desk in an American up-market gadgets-cum-furniture store. But it was of a heavy dark wood that would not at all fit in the teahouse/study. He visited the shop a few days

The japonica quince budding and blooming, with the mahogany strip at the top.

later, measured it up, drew the design, and reproduced it in the same fir as we had used for the window surrounds and the borders of the tatami mats.

The fir is appropriate, apart from also being beautiful, because it comes from local Douglas fir trees. They are named for David Douglas, a Scotsman who was enormously tough. The fir named after him was one of 200 species he was the

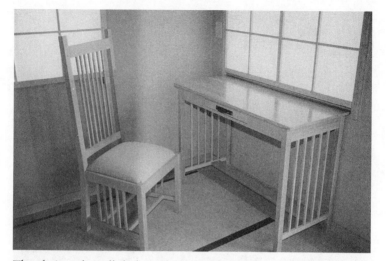

The chair and small desk, with the shoji screens in place over the windows. Brendan built the screens to fit exactly over the window surrounds. The one above the table is hinged in the middle and can be lifted off, folded, and stood beside the desk when the sun is not too bright. We will add a clear plastic base, so that the legs of the table and chair will not sit on the tatami.

first Westerner to collect and describe and whose seeds he sent back to the Royal Horticultural Society in London. His passion for natural history developed early apparently. As a schoolboy, he received a penny a day for his lunch, and was found to be spending it on food for a nest of owls. While exploring the fauna of the West Coast forests, he expressed deep concern for the likely impact on the native people of those he knew would follow him. He died in Hawaii in 1834 at the age of thirty-five, probably murdered for the small amount of money he was carrying.

A small extension to the garden
I can see now that I have given myself a never-ending task, or, better, a kind of companion that seems always pleased when I do a bit of work with it. The gardening will go on though the

book has to finish. My wife is sufficiently charmed by the Japanese-style invasion at the rear to authorize extending it a little in front of the teahouse/study, particularly to cover the area of lawn that has been destroyed during its building. So I bought some more basalt stones, gravel, and bamboo from my friends at the landscape supply center, and toured familiar nurseries for a few plants. It took little time to make a small garden, and I even moved into it the pom-pom juniper that began its career up by the bog. You can perhaps make it out on the left of the picture. You may also be able to just make out a slightly fluffy patch above the three stones in the gravel. That patch is a rather exotic moss, which I fear may not survive. My wife and I "rescued" it from one of our provincial parks.

Before you contact the Mounties, I should explain. My wife and I took a long weekend recently on Vancouver Island and visited a couple of magnificent local parks. One of our favorite spots is Englishman River Falls, and another is Little Qualicum Falls. Both were roaring with spring waters, and their spray as they dived into canyons rose into rainbows above our heads. The rocks and trees all around were covered with frothy blankets of a frilly moss, within which grew strong bright ferns. I kept mumbling to my wife how bits of this would look great in the garden at home. She dragged me away whenever I seemed in danger of bending down toward it with nefarious intent. But then fate took a hand. In front of us in the path was a long piece of the moss. It had grown too heavy for the tree up which it had been crawling and had fallen off, perhaps helped by last night's winds, waiting for someone like me to come along and help it get rerooted somewhere in our garden.

But, despite the evident hand of Providence, my wife was reluctant to be seen with us carrying such a bundle to the car, as it would inevitably look as though we were mossnappers. The bundle was like an old feather boa that a dowager might have tossed around her ample shoulders. My wife relented,

The small continuation of the garden in front of the teahouse/study.
To the right is a maple. The stones on which the steps rest are
Tumbled Pennsylvania Bluestone, and very handsome they look.
The small plant among the three stones in the gravel is a lavender.

and we sneaked it into the trunk of the car without being seen.
I think she was even more delighted with it than I was when
we took it out of the car at the cabin where we were staying,
watering it to keep it moist for the next couple of days before
we went home. But, of course, this single strip wouldn't look
very good by itself, would it? The next day, for our trip to
Little Qualicum Falls, my wife took a large plastic bag with
her and a spoon. When we found ourselves again surrounded
by acres of the moss, she began poking around with the spoon.
We agreed that we could sneak a bit more only from areas that
were out of sight of the paths; we also wanted some with small
ferns growing through it.

A view from under an apple tree, with cherry blossoms hanging over the near window. The white bulk of Moby Rock sits patiently to the right of the pond.

So we did indeed become criminal mossnappers, and fern-nappers, though only in a very small way. I am as shocked telling you this as you are no doubt in reading it. This is how all careers in crime begin. Intoxicated with the desire for something, one justifies the criminal act to oneself and indulges only in a tiny theft that will hurt no one. My shock in remembering this affront to human decency will, I hope, inoculate me against any further crimes of this sort. But, who knows— next it'll be maidenhair ferns in the summer, then bushes, then trees, and soon I'll be dragging forests home!

After I had planted the rescued and stolen moss and ferns in this small extension of the garden in front of the teahouse/study,

Looking down on the bog and over the Japanese black pine at the finished teahouse/study.

I looked around for the next job, and felt for a moment disoriented. There was no further job to do. The garden and its teahouse/study were finished. I felt a little bereft, as though deserted by a partner whose presence I had taken for granted. What was I to do now?

I will spend the odd hour hand-picking leaves and plucking blades of grass from the moss, netting uninvited floating bits from the pond, moving the odd stone now and then, and generally pottering. But mostly, I hope, I will sit at the desk and glance up now and then to look out the window at it all, mildly surprised to find it there.

Along with the two final pictures of the more or less completed Japanese garden and its teahouse/study, here is one of Mike planting a stone from Tanya's garden, which started this small adventure.

Mike placing a stone from Tanya's garden. He took back to Japan a stone from mine.

Conclusion

We must laugh and we must sing,
We are blest by everything,
Everything we look upon is blest.
— *W. B. Yeats*

I SIT LOOKING THROUGH
the teahouse window up into the sky, and see a bird, resting on a slight rising breeze, perhaps bemused by this pond's reflection of the blue above it. The bird slides sideways down the wind to pass close over the surface and inspect the pond's possible contribution to its diet, and is gone in a flash across neighboring gardens. Whenever I look out at the garden, my eye moves first to the stream, where the water from the bog runs through multicolored stones toward the fall into the pond. Friends donated many of the stones that are gathered here to make the water gurgle. There are pebbles from Japan, Hong Kong, England, Romania, Portugal, Ireland, Hawaii, Texas, Haida Gwaii, Toronto, Masada, Oxford, Washington — as well as a set of green stones from the beach on Vancouver Island where we used to take the children when they were little. And Mike's pebble from Tanya's balcony garden in Nagoya.

Before me on the desk are files with slips of paper of various sizes and colors. There are notes of measurements I can no longer decipher, and amounts of money for quantities of wood or stone, and lists of things to do, happily long done:

Order more basalt, 2/2.5 tons? Ask Gary at yard.
Mini-ferns, Korean.
Bags of gravel, granite, light.
Moby Rock—out. pulley?
Bamboo fertilizer 10-6-4.
Fill behind wall.
Two-needle black pine? For up by bog.
Think what size teahouse? Maybe just covered bench?

They are in a file marked "Gardening Info," into which I also tossed all the labels from the plants I bought, many of them those printed plastic things stuck into the soil at the edge of the pot. These were put into the file with bits of soil attached, and so my lists are stained and mostly crumpled from having gone with me on the errands they describe, to be stuffed into a pocket once I had followed their instructions. They have a dirty authenticity.

And would I do it all again, knowing what work would be involved? I think so. And what have I learned from all this? Beats me, as the British poet Philip Larkin wrote, distilling the lessons he had gathered from his experience. Maybe something about this cooperative battle with nature that we don't expect to win. And that we are only undefeated as long as we go on trying. I'll think about it in the teahouse, watching the waterfall and the ripples it makes on the pond, and the reflection the late sun casts from them onto the fence, or when the light fails on a winter's afternoon and the bamboo minutely shrugs in the window.

Some people tell me I must feel a sense of accomplishment. But I really don't. And I can't quite see this small garden and its teahouse as something I have done. Nietzsche, that fierce but entertaining philosopher, suggested that our usual way of thinking of ourselves as originators of actions is simply an illusion produced by our language. We have nouns for agents and verbs for what they do. But our relationship to the world isn't one of noun to verb. I don't *feel* like a noun, and the garden doesn't look like my verb.

You may be familiar with Chuang Tzu's most famous semi-humorous observation: "While he is dreaming he does not know it is a dream, and in his dream he may even try to interpret a dream. Only after he wakes does he know it was a dream. And someday there will be a great awakening when we know this is all a great dream." A similar idea was expressed around the same time a long way away by that other mystic, poet, and jokester, Plato. He suggested that the everyday world around us is like shadows on a wall in front of our eyes. But the shadows are cast by a reality that we cannot see.

The choices of what stones to use and where to put them were mine, in some sense, but in some sense, too, they were not *mine*. Something hidden from us urges one choice rather than another, one aesthetic principle rather than another. Something that is part of the baggage that comes with us, in our genes and from our upbringing, does much of the choosing for us. The garden is one of the things that has happened to happen, and I have been a somewhat bemused instrument in its construction.

So my feeling about the finished garden is something of a mixture of Eastern Zen and Western irony coming together. Irony shows us that our intentions and our actions are in no simple sense our own, while Zen encourages us to suppress the sense of self as agent entirely. I suppose I am failing a tad in both by being glad the garden has happened to happen to me. And, anyway, my failures in irony and Zen will themselves soon be as nothing. Moby Rock will see all that now surrounds it, the moss and plants and the teahouse across the

A poppy in the alcove.

pond, decay and vanish between the slow beats of its granite heart. The Zen stance before the world and its passing fancies requires recognition that "the inclination toward nothingness is unrelenting and universal." But, while Western irony reaches its own recognition of this, it is more buoyant, perhaps, and encourages us also to bear in mind that there is a present in which there is something. And while we should be attentive to the slide toward nothingness and to the scale of time in which Moby Rock too will crumble, we should not be so intent on that austere dimension that we fail to delight in our present abundance of somethings.